A Cloud
of
Witnesses

DEDICATION

For Rev. Ann Cornelia Partner
a woman of sacred service

A CLOUD
of
WITNESSES

READINGS ON WOMEN OF FAITH

MARGARET & DANIEL PARTNER

Fleming H. Revell
A Division of Baker Book House Co
Grand Rapids, Michigan 49516

© 2000 by Margaret and Daniel Partner

Published by Fleming H. Revell
a division of Baker Book House Company
P.O. Box 6287, Grand Rapids, MI 49516-6287

Printed in the United States of America

ISBN 0-8007-5734-3

Library of Congress Cataloging-in-Publication Data is on file at the Library of Congress, Washington, D. C.

Scripture quotations are from the New Revised Standard Version of the Bible, copyright 1989 by the Division of Christian Education of the National Council of the Churches of Christ in the USA. Used by permission.

For current information about all releases from Baker Book House, visit our web site:
http://www.bakerbooks.com

CONTENTS

5

PART 3 THE WIVES AND MOTHERS

PART 4 THE MARTYRS

PART 5 THE POETS

PART 6 THE PROPHETS

PART 7 THE WRITERS

A PRAYER
FOR GOD'S SERVANTS

Heavenly Father, whose blessed Son came not to be served but
to serve: Bless all who, following in his steps, give themselves to
the service of others; that with wisdom, patience, and courage,
they may minister in his Name to the suffering, the friendless,
and the needy; for the love of him who laid down his life for us,
your Son our Savior Jesus Christ, who lives and reigns with you
and the Holy Spirit, one God, for ever and ever. Amen.

FROM *THE BOOK OF COMMON PRAYER*

INTRODUCTION

One day long ago, a woman carried a basket down to a river. In the basket lay her infant son. Leaving the basket to float at the river's edge, the woman went away while her daughter stayed behind, watching from a distance. The baby in the basket floating in the Nile River—the boy who would come to be known as Moses—represents the life of the woman who set him afloat (Exodus 2:1–10). She is one of untold millions of women who have committed their lives to God by faith. Very few of these stories have been recorded in any way. Some, like the story of Moses' mother, are recorded in the Bible. Others are written in history books. Some live on in memory, but most are long forgotten.

When the Bible tells of the people of faith, it says that the world was not worthy of them and calls them a great cloud of witnesses that is surrounding us (Hebrews 11:38; 12:1). Our book introduces some women who are now among the people gathered in this great cloud.

Yet we would like to steer you away from a pitfall that awaits those who read about such people. We tend to compare ourselves with these marvelous people of faith. When making such a comparison, our experience is that we do not feel we measure up to the level of love and commitment to God seen in such lives. This is the trap of self-reproach. But should we compare our lives to theirs? Is this the reason their stories are preserved for us? No. We present this book to encourage you to press on toward the goal to which God has called you (Philippians 3:14).

Those of us who have embarked on a life of faith are like that mother long ago who entrusted her life to God as she left a basket at the river's edge. Surrounded by a great cloud of witnesses, we are daily seeking the way to proceed. In the New Testament Book of Hebrews the apostle Paul says that we should "throw off everything that hinders and the sin that so easily entangles." He continues, "let us run with perseverance the race marked out for us" (12:1).

"And how," you rightly ask, "can I possibly do this?"

All believers, including those who are named in *A Cloud of Witnesses*, have only been able to run the race while looking to Jesus, the author and perfecter of their faith. He alone endured death on a cross and, refusing to be put to shame by such a miserable death, resurrected from the grave. Now he is seated "at the right hand of the throne of God" (Hebrews 12:2). Paul continues, "consider him who endured such opposition from sinful men, so that you will not grow weary and lose heart" (v. 3).

Therefore, we pray that as you read about these women of faith, you will follow the gaze of their eyes, heed the Lord's glory, and so be "transformed into his likeness with ever-increasing glory" (2 Corinthians 3:18).

Margaret and Daniel Partner
September 2000

PART 1

THE
WORKERS

SELINA HASTINGS, COUNTESS OF HUNTINGDON

(1707–1791)

> The more scriptural and simple your sermons and to the heart, the better. Apply to facts, with the knowledge of evils in your heart. That is the truth our Lord must bless. He can witness to nothing else, as he essentially and emphatically is truth itself. . . . I write thus, hoping and believing that you have counted the cost, and that you truly mean to devote yourself unreservedly to the Lord Jesus Christ.
>
> To ministerial students at Trevecca House, Talgarth, South Wales, 1768

In the days when the Church of England denied Methodist preachers access to the pulpit, Selina Hastings, Countess of Huntingdon, became their patron. Selina was the daughter of the second Earl of Ferrers and granddaughter of the Speaker of the House of Commons. In 1728 she married Theophilus Hastings, ninth Earl of Huntingdon; together they had four sons and three daughters.

To the dismay of her well-born friends, in 1731, Lady Huntingdon joined the controversial Methodists. Widowed at the age of thirty-nine, she withdrew further from the aristocracy and devoted herself to the service of the gospel, following a long tradition of Christian women.

This tradition began early, when, in addition to the twelve disciples, several women were with Jesus Christ, notably Joanna, the wife of the steward to Herod, the Roman king of Judea. As steward, Joanna's husband was manager of the royal household—a position of wealth and power. Joanna used her share of this wealth to provide for Christ and his disciples (Luke 8:2–3). Similarly, Lady Huntingdon took clergymen to preach throughout the British Isles, financed more than sixty chapels and a seminary in

South Wales, and sponsored the work of George Whitefield—the dominant evangelist of the day.

The Methodist Revival caused great tumult in England. Riots often threatened the lives of John Wesley and his followers. Although it was an evangelistic order within the Church of England, Methodism was never appreciated or approved by the church hierarchy. Church doors everywhere were closed to its preachers. John Wesley was even locked out at Epworth, where his father, an Anglican priest, had devoted forty years in service to God. So in the churchyard at Epworth Wesley used his father's tomb as a platform from which to preach.

Can you imagine the aristocratic gossip that arose when Lady Huntingdon began to spend her wealth in support of the Methodists? She lived in the ancient mansion of her husband's family, Donnington Hall; she was a member of British high society, a beautiful woman, a lady of breeding, born to authority.

But Lady Huntingdon believed that "if God came near to Abraham and Moses, why should he not come near to these new servants [the Methodists]? Why should not the same light that shone on Mount Sinai . . . and upon Saul on his way to Damascus manifest itself in England today?" And for this end she did all she could, becoming like the first-century deacon Phoebe, "a benefactor of many and of [the apostle] as well" (Romans 16:2).

A half century of supporting the work of the gospel drained Lady Huntingdon's considerable resources. She obtained donations for the work from wealthy friends, sold her jewels, and moved to more humble living quarters. With the Wesleys and Whitefield, Lady Huntingdon was among the leaders of the early Methodists. Outliving them all, she wrote in her will, "The grand view and desire of my life has been the good of all mankind."

Lord, thank you for the example of generosity seen in Joanna, Phoebe, and Lady Huntingdon. I ask not only that I could follow in their steps but that you would find people of much greater means than I who would gladly become benefactors of the gospel.

RELATED SCRIPTURE READING—MARK 12:41–44

ISABELLA GRAHAM

(1742–1814)

Oh you who are Alpha and Omega, . . . write with power, speak with power, in the heart of the angel of this church. Have you not in former days had your dwelling among them [the churches]? In days of trouble did you not work in them the fruits of labor and patience so that for your name's sake they labored and fainted not? You blessed them and gave them peace. . . . Alas, Lord, we have . . . left our first love; we have not watched and prayed as you gave us command; . . .

"Your covenant is well ordered in all things and it is sure." Here, O Lord, I take my stand; here I lay my foundation, and on this your covenant I build; or rather here you yourself have laid my foundation, and on this rock you have set my soul and built my hopes, you subduing my enmity, I acquiesce. I will now "remember the years of your right hand."

FROM DEVOTIONAL EXERCISES, 1819

Do you ever wonder how to pray? Perhaps you feel so meek or shy that you avoid speaking prayer aloud. Do you sometimes feel your prayers are impotent, redundant, pedantic, perfunctory— just plain useless? Take a hint from the journal of Isabella Graham, who knew a great secret of prayer. Her journal (*Devotional Exercises*, 1819) is a classic of prayer and devotional thought.

In the short selection from her journal quoted here, Graham is praying. But she does not use her own words. Instead she alludes to many verses of Scripture; some she quotes outright. The first paragraph begins with the Lord's name in Revelation 1:8. The prayer continues by drawing from the Lord's rebuke of the churches in chapters 2 and 3.

The worshiper shifts to 2 Samuel 23:5 as she begins a new thought, then embarks on words and sentiments so rich that they must have been drawn from a storehouse of Scripture in her heart. Graham then repeats the words of an afflicted psalmist as her vow to the Lord—I will now "remember the years of your right hand" (see Psalm 77:10).

Scottish church worker Isabella Graham married John Graham, a British Army surgeon, in 1765. Together they were stationed at Fort Niagara, New York. After her husband's death in Antigua, Graham returned to Scotland in 1773 and taught primary school to support her children.

About 1790 Graham returned to New York, organized a school, and founded the Society for the Relief of Poor Widows with Small Children. She helped to found other charities for the disfranchised of society including the poor, the homeless, and prisoners. Soon after Graham's death, her daughter, Joanna Graham Bethune, was instrumental in founding the American Sunday School Union, the first such organization in this country.

Isabella Graham was evidently steeped in the Word of God. It seems to flow out of her as she prays. It fortifies her prayer with meaning and power. The wonderful fact is that anyone, you or I, can pray in this way. Human ideas and eloquence (or lack thereof) can never match the beauty and weight of the Word of God in prayer. Try praying the words of Scripture, which is brimful of human hope and godly faith:

> When I was a child, I spoke like a child, I thought like a child, I reasoned like a child; when I became an adult, I put an end to childish ways. For now we see in a mirror, dimly, but then we will see face to face. Now I know only in part; then I will know fully, even as I have been fully known.

1 CORINTHIANS 13:11–12

Heavenly Father, thank you for the Bible. May it be to me as it was to your prophet Jeremiah who found your words and knew their taste. They became the joy and rejoicing of his heart.

RELATED SCRIPTURE READING—JEREMIAH 15:16

ELIZABETH SETON

(1774–1821)

Life-giving heavenly bread, feed me, sanctify me, reign in me, transform me to yourself, live in me, and let me live in you . . . listen to you as to my master, obey you as my king, imitate you as my model, follow you as my shepherd, love you as my father, see you as my physician who will heal all the maladies of my soul. Be indeed my way, truth, and life. Sustain me, O heavenly manna, through the desert of this world till I shall behold you unveiled in your glory.

A PRAYER OF ELIZABETH SETON

The American educator and philanthropist Elizabeth Ann (Bayley) Seton was born in New York City to a well-to-do family. She was well educated by her father, a professor at Columbia College. In 1794 Elizabeth married William Seton, a successful merchant. With her sister-in-law, Rebecca Seton, Elizabeth worked so diligently in city charities that people called them the "Protestant Sisters of Charity."

Seton's father-in-law died in 1798, and Elizabeth and William Seton, themselves with five children, were left to care for his large orphaned family. In 1803 William Seton suffered a reversal of fortune, and his health began to fail. Elizabeth accompanied him to Italy in hope of recovery there, but William died of tuberculosis in Pisa. Elizabeth remained in Italy until 1804 and while there was attracted to the Catholic Church.

Returning to New York, Seton entered a time of spiritual perplexity. Her subsequent conversion to Catholicism in 1805 raised a storm of protest among her Protestant relatives and friends, but it also began her life's work.

In 1808 she opened a school for girls near the chapel of St. Mary's Seminary in Baltimore. Soon helpers joined her, and the little school for the daughters of the wealthy prospered. In 1809,

with funds from a Virginia seminarian, Seton established an institution for teaching poor children in Emmitsburg, Maryland. This
marked the beginning of parochial education in the United States.
The school at Emmitsburg was the first of what later grew into a
religious community known as the American Sisters of Charity.
Today the order is composed of thirteen congregations and has
seven thousand members around the world.

Seton died of tuberculosis sixteen years after becoming a
Catholic, but the years of her labor were very fruitful. This was
all the more remarkable because of the many trials she had in
her life. She was cut off from her family who disagreed with her
denominational choice and, as a result, became a refugee from
her home in New York. Also, after the death of her husband,
four of Seton's children preceded her in death. But she was better educated than most women of her time and so she took what
she had—her education—and educated others.

The prayer quoted here tells us something about Elizabeth
Seton's faith. It reveals her subjective knowledge of Christ—the
life-giving, heavenly bread—who will feed and sanctify, reign
over and transform those who will allow this. Seton's desire to
let God live in her and to live in God expresses the core purpose
of Christ's redemption. She wanted to hear the master, obey the
king, imitate the model, follow the shepherd, love the father, and
have her soul healed by the physician. This is how to walk on
the way, live in the truth, and enjoy the life who is Jesus Christ.

Elizabeth Seton used her energy to serve God. She could have
been like some of the people in Jesus' day who were satisfied to
say, "We have Abraham as our ancestor" (Luke 3:8). In other
words, Seton could have rested in the comfort of her family in
New York or entered the established structure of her church. But
she did not. Rather, she bore fruits worthy of her repentance (v. 8).

*Sustain me, O heavenly manna, through the desert of this world till
I shall behold you unveiled in your glory.*

RELATED SCRIPTURE READING—LUKE 3:9–14

ELIZABETH FRY

(1780–1845)

> O Lord, may I be directed what to do and what to leave undone; and then may I humbly trust that a blessing will be with me in my various engagements. . . . Enable me, O Lord, to feel tenderly and charitably toward all my beloved fellow mortals. . . . Let me walk in all humility and Godly fear before all men, and in thy sight.
>
> A PRAYER OF ELIZABETH FRY

The Christian church is sometimes accused of fomenting violence and bringing death to the world. Critics may point to the Crusades or the excesses of extremist fundamentalists as illustrations. But history shows too that mercy and justice were introduced to this world through the Judeo-Christian tradition. Begin with the many injunctions for justice in the ancient Hebrew Scriptures: "You shall not render an unjust judgment; you shall not be partial to the poor or defer to the great: with justice you shall judge your neighbor" (Leviticus 19:15). Then consider God's condemnation of the people for ignoring justice: "I will not revoke the punishment; because they sell the righteous for silver, and the needy for a pair of sandals—they who trample the head of the poor into the dust of the earth, and push the afflicted out of the way" (Amos 2:6–7).

And consider where social reform entered our culture: through the hearts and labors of the Christian inheritors of the Jewish tradition of justice. Elizabeth Fry is just one of tens of thousands of Christians, known and unknown, who labored and labor still to bring mercy and justice to earth.

In 1813 the English Quaker Elizabeth Fry began to minister to the women in Newgate Prison by reading aloud to them from the Bible. At that time there were three hundred women in the prison living with numerous children in four small rooms without beds, bedding, or other comforts.

In 1816 Fry, mother of eleven children, formed the Association for the Improvement of the Female Prisoner in Newgate and began to institute England's first prison reforms. The association provided the prisoners with clothing, employment, instruction in the Bible and other subjects, and training in social skills. Fry's success was so dramatic that city authorities adopted for the prison the rules she formulated. These are considered the first principles of modern prison management.

Fry and her associates visited every convict ship as it left London, praying with the women prisoners before they sailed to the penal settlements in Australia. But there was more than prayer. Fry saw to it that the women had materials for work during the voyage. The women could support themselves by the sale of the finished articles in Australia.

Fry traveled throughout the British Isles and the Continent in the interest of prison reform. She was active in the care of the homeless, insane, and diseased, providing for libraries for coastguardsmen, the training of nurses, and more. She once prophetically told the King of France, with typical Quaker directness, "When thee builds a prison thee had better build with the thought ever in mind that thee and thy children may occupy the cells."

U.S. congressman from Virginia John Randolph visited England in 1822 and wrote the following in a letter to a friend:

> I have seen, sir, Elizabeth Fry, in Newgate, and I have witnessed there, sir, miraculous effects of true Christianity upon the most depraved of human beings—bad women, sir, who are worse if possible, than the Devil himself. And yet the wretched outcasts have been tamed and subdued by the Christian eloquence of Mrs. Fry. Nothing but religion can effect this miracle, sir.

O Lord, who is righteous and who loves righteous deeds, I pray that you will hear the desire of the meek and strengthen their heart. Hear their prayers and do justice for the orphan and the oppressed.

RELATED SCRIPTURE READING—PSALM 33:4–5

CATHERINE BOOTH

(1829–1890)

There are thousands talking about his second coming who will neither see nor receive him in the person of his humble and persecuted followers. No. They are looking for him in the clouds! What a sensation there would be if he were to come again in a carpenter's coat. How many would recognize him then, I wonder? I am afraid it would be the old story, "Crucify him!" . . . Oh for grace always to see him where he is to be seen, for verily, flesh and blood do not reveal this unto us! Well, bless the Lord, I keep seeing him risen again in the forms of drunkards and ruffians of all descriptions.

FROM A LETTER BY CATHERINE BOOTH

Catherine Booth is known as the mother of the Salvation Army. In 1855 Catherine married William Booth, a Methodist minister. Together they had eight children, all of whom became active in the Salvation Army. Catherine was an influential preacher and advanced the right of women to preach the gospel. William Booth was accused of elevating women to man's status because women in the Salvation Army enjoyed equal rights with men. He later said that "the best men in my Army are the women." The Booths saw clearly that in Christ there is neither male nor female. They said that in the gospel, like nature, both sexes have complete mental and spiritual equality.

Mrs. Booth was highly active in social reform. In 1885 she took part in the campaign that secured the passing of the Criminal Law Amendment Act, designed to protect young girls. In this capacity she appealed in a letter to Queen Victoria that crimes against women were undermining the social fabric and "would bring down the judgments of God upon our nation." She informed British Prime Minister Gladstone that the House of Commons was so absorbed with matters of property and taxes that it had no time to be concerned about the destruction of England's womanhood.

In the excerpt quoted here, Mrs. Booth says that people "neither see nor receive [Christ] in the person of his humble and persecuted followers." An interesting Bible story explains this:

Saul of Tarsus thought he could put an end to an aberrant sect of Judaism, which he himself later called the Way (Acts 24:14). "I not only locked up many of the saints in prison," he testified, "but I also cast my vote against them when they were being condemned to death. . . . I tried to force them to blaspheme; and . . . I pursued them even to foreign cities" (26:10–11).

One of these cities was Damascus. As Saul was traveling there, "at midday . . . I heard a voice saying to me in the Hebrew language, 'Saul, Saul, why are you persecuting me?' . . . I asked, 'Who are you, Lord?' The Lord answered, 'I am Jesus whom you are persecuting'" (vv. 13–15).

Saul (later called Paul) thought he was persecuting people who believed in Jesus Christ. In fact he was persecuting Jesus Christ himself. This story illustrates two very basic truths of the gospel. First, those who believe in Christ are indeed *in* Christ. Paul repeats this fact again and again in his epistles (see Romans 6:3; 1 Corinthians 1:2; Ephesians 1:1; 1 Thessalonians 1:1). Second, when you believe in Christ, you have Christ *in you*. This reality is also frequently repeated in Paul's writing (see Romans 8:10; 2 Corinthians 13:5; Galatians 2:20; Colossians 1:27).

We don't have to worry that Christ will come again in a carpenter's coat, as Booth imagined. The truth is, Christ comes to you in his believers, and his believers come to you in Christ. Booth is right. She simply asks that we all look for Christ in others and view them in Christ. Then, with God's mercy, we may recognize him at his final advent.

Heavenly Father, I ask that I may clearly see the great mystery of the ages. Open my heart to savor the riches of the glory of this mystery, which is Christ in me and Christ in others, the hope of glory.

RELATED SCRIPTURE READING—COLOSSIANS 1:25–27

DOROTHY DAY

(1897–1980)

For a total Christian, the goad of duty is not needed—always prodding one to perform this or that good deed. It is not a duty to help Christ, it is a privilege. Is it likely that Martha and Mary sat back and considered that they had done all that was expected of them—is it likely that Peter's mother-in-law grudgingly served the chicken she had meant to keep till Sunday because she thought it was her "duty"? She did it gladly; she would have served ten chickens if she had them.

If that is the way they gave hospitality to Christ, it is certain that is the way it should still be given. Not for the sake of humanity. Not because it might be Christ who stays with us, comes to see us, takes up our time. Not because these people remind us of Christ . . . but because they *are* Christ, asking us to find room for him, exactly as he did at the first Christmas.

FROM *THE LONG LONELINESS*

Brooklyn-born Dorothy Day founded the Catholic Worker movement in 1932 after observing a hunger march in Washington, D.C. There she sympathetically watched the protesters parade, but she could not join the activities because the Communist Party, organizers of the march, opposed capitalism *and* religion.

"I offered up a special prayer," she recalled, "that some way would open up for me to use what talents I possessed for my fellow workers, for the poor." Out of this desire a newspaper was published to promulgate Catholic social teaching and promote steps to bring about society's peaceful transformation. On May 1, 1932, the first copies of the *Catholic Worker* were sold for a penny apiece—100,000 monthly copies were being printed by the end of the year. The paper addressed "those who worked with hand or brain, those who did physical, mental or spiritual work . . . the poor, the dispossessed, the exploited" and called for readers' personal commitment to change.

Dorothy Day's work grew out of the Great Depression and today there are more than 140 Catholic Worker communities. Like their founder, the members practice nonviolence, voluntary poverty, hospitality to the homeless, and a testimony of protest against injustice, war, racism, and violence of all forms. The *Catholic Worker* is still published and still costs a penny a copy.

Dorothy Day's fellow worker was Peter Maurin, a French priest who embraced poverty and lived a simple, celibate life. With a vision of a social order steeped in the basic values of the gospel, Maurin took literally the words of Jesus: "I was a stranger and you took me in." His essays in the *Catholic Worker* encouraged the Christian practice of hospitality to those who were homeless. Homeless people soon arrived at Day's apartment, and she and Maurin began to put their principles into practice.

As Day says, a Christian does not need "the goad of duty." Serving others is an automatic response of our new life in Christ. This is why the people who are rewarded with the heavenly kingdom seem unaware that they deserve it (see Matthew 25:31–40). Puzzled, they ask Christ, "When was it that we saw you a stranger and welcomed you, or naked and gave you clothing?" (v. 38).

When we as Christians see a need, the impulse is to help. This impulse does not arise out of a sense of duty; it is the spontaneous response of the new life we received when we first believed.

Dorothy Day is a model of the gospel qualities that testify of the resurrected Christ. Yet holiness, service, suffering, justice, and charity were not her qualities, nor are they yours or mine. These qualities uniquely express Christ who lives in us.

Father God, I know that I have been crucified with Christ and it is no longer I who live, but Christ lives in me. So I earnestly pray that the life I now live in the flesh would be lived by faith in the Son of God, who loved me and gave himself for me.

RELATED SCRIPTURE READING—GALATIANS 2:20

MOTHER TERESA

(1910–1997)

I do not understand why some people are . . . denying the beautiful differences between men and women. . . . God has created each one of us, every human being, for greater things—to love and to be loved. But why did God make some of us men and others women? Because a woman's love is one image of the love of God, and a man's love is another image of God's love. Both are created to love, but each in a different way. Woman and man complete each other, and together show forth God's love more fully than either can do alone.

FROM A SPEECH BY MOTHER TERESA

The Christian faith is rooted in a single act of love: "God so loved the world that he gave his only Son, so that everyone who believes in him may not perish but may have eternal life" (John 3:16). Is it too much, then, to expect that faith will prosper only through similar sacrificial love?

Christ and his apostles unanimously echoed the Old Testament exhortation to love your neighbor as yourself (Leviticus 19:18; Matthew 22:39; Romans 13:9; Galatians 5:14; James 2:8). The Bible teaches love for strangers and for enemies and that we must work for the good of all (Galatians 6:10).

Born in Yugoslavia, Agnes Gonxha Bojaxhiu followed this scriptural exhortation. She joined the Sisters of Loreto in 1928 and took her name from Teresa de Lisieux, who emphasized joy in menial tasks. In 1948 Mother Teresa began a new ministry to the very poor—the Missionaries of Charity. This work eventually included a home for the dying, an orphanage, a leper colony, an employment workshop, various medical centers, and countless shelters. In 1965 the ministry began to spread to Venezuela,

Ceylon, Tanzania, Rome, Cuba, and other locations, each making good on Mother Teresa's call to serve the "poorest of the poor."

When Mother Teresa of Calcutta founded the Missionaries of Charity, she said, "I realized that I had the call to take care of the sick and the dying, the hungry, the naked, the homeless— to be God's love in action to the poorest of the poor."

"There is a terrible hunger for love," she once said. "We all experience that in our lives—the pain, the loneliness. We must have the courage to recognize it. The poor you may have right in your own family. Find them. Love them. Put your love for them in living action. For in loving them, you are loving God himself."

The beating heart of the gospel is 1 Corinthians 13. Sometimes called "The Song of Love," it is the final word on the subject of love. Everything is valueless without love, it says (vv. 1–3). Love is patient, kind, not envious or boastful or arrogant or rude. Love does not "insist on its own way; it is not irritable or resentful; it does not rejoice in wrongdoing, but rejoices in the truth. It bears all things, believes all things, hopes all things, endures all things" (vv. 4–7). In other words, love is utterly selfless. So it endures throughout eternity (vv. 8–10) and is the unique and ultimate expression of Christian maturity (vv. 11–12)—the highest of all virtues (v. 13).

Is such love humanly possible? Only through the knowledge of God can such love be realized, because, "whoever does not love does not know God, for God is love. God's love was revealed among us in this way: God sent his only Son into the world so that we might live through him" (1 John 4:8–9).

God, of your goodness, give me yourself for you are sufficient for me. I cannot properly ask anything less, to be worthy of you. If I were to ask less, I should always be in want. In you alone do I have all.

A PRAYER OF JULIAN OF NORWICH

RELATED SCRIPTURE READING—1 JOHN 4:20–21

PART 2

THE
PREACHERS
AND
MISSIONARIES

SOJOURNER TRUTH

(CA. 1797–1883)

Isabella avers that, in her darkest hours, she had no fear of any worse hell than the one she then carried in her bosom; though it had ever been pictured to her in its deepest colors, and threatened her as a reward for all her misdemeanors. . . . Her faith in prayer is equal to her faith in the love of Jesus. Her language is, "Let others say what they will of the efficacy of prayer, I believe in it, and I shall pray. Thank God! Yes, I *shall always pray*," she exclaims, putting her hands together with the greatest enthusiasm. . . .

While in deep affliction, she labored for the recovery of her son, she prayed with constancy and fervor; and the following may be taken as a specimen: "Oh, God, you know how much I am distressed, for I have told you again and again. Now, God, help me get my son. If you were in trouble, as I am, and I could help you, as you can me, think I wouldn't do it? Yes, God, you *know* I would do it. Oh, God, you know I have no money, but you can make the people do for me, and you must make the people do for me. I will never give you peace till you do, God. Oh, God, make the people hear me—don't let them turn me off, without hearing and helping me."

FROM *THE NARRATIVE OF SOJOURNER TRUTH*

In this selection Sojourner Truth refers to her court battle through which she would recover her small son, who had been sold illegally into slavery. Don't you think Truth's prayer is refreshing? She seems to have been willing to bargain with God: "If you were in trouble, as I am, and I could help you, as you can me, think I wouldn't do it? Yes, God, you *know* I would do it." Truth doesn't presume to think that she can do anything for God. She simply says that she would if she could.

Abraham once struck a bargain with God (see Genesis 18:22–33). The foundation of his argument is one we can still use today. God was on the way to destroy Sodom, and Abraham reminded him that there might be righteous citizens of Sodom who would also be destroyed. "Shall not the Judge of all the earth do what is just?" he asked (v. 25). The patriarch used God's righteousness as a bargaining chip on behalf of the righteous.

Another way to bargain in prayer is to remind God of his promises. After all, Scripture says, "The promise is for you" (Acts 2:39). All the promises have been enacted by the death and resurrection of Jesus Christ and delivered by the promised Holy Spirit. Through the promises we know that "everyone who calls on the name of the Lord shall be saved" (v. 21).

Sojourner Truth was born a slave in Ulster County, New York. She began to preach in 1843 and, using Scripture for support, became an outspoken preacher against slavery and for the rights of women.

Isabella Van Wagener was the given name of the woman eventually known as Sojourner Truth. She was the abused chattel of several masters until New York abolished slavery in 1827. About 1829 she became a domestic in New York City where she lived with her two youngest children. There she became associated with the zealous religious missionary Elijah Pierson, and she obeyed a supernatural call to "travel up and down the land." She left New York in 1843, took the name Sojourner Truth, and through singing, preaching, and debating, spread the message of God's goodness and the brotherhood of man.

Thank you, Lord, for the simple faith of Sojourner Truth and others like her. Strengthen my faith to believe your promises and appropriate them in prayer.

RELATED SCRIPTURE READING—JOEL 2:28–29; ACTS 1:4–5

SOJOURNER TRUTH

A SPEECH

At a women's rights convention in Akron, Ohio, Sojourner Truth spoke to challenge the prevailing notions of what, at that time, it meant to be a woman. The director of the convention, Frances D. Gage, later recounted the speech. We present it here with no further comments besides those of Ms. Gage.

Slowly from her seat in the corner rose Sojourner Truth, who, till now, had scarcely lifted her head. "Don't let her speak!" gasped half a dozen in my ear. She moved slowly and solemnly to the front, laid her old bonnet at her feet, and turned her great, speaking eyes to me. There was a hissing sound of disapprobation above and below. I rose and announced "Sojourner Truth," and begged the audience to keep silence for a few moments. The tumult subsided at once, and every eye was fixed on this almost Amazon form, which stood nearly six feet high, head erect, and eye piercing the upper air, like one in a dream. At her first word, there was a profound hush. She spoke in deep tones, which, though not loud, reached every ear in the house, and away through the throng at the doors and windows:

Well, chilern, whar dar is so much racket dar must be something out o'kilter. . . . Dat man ober dar say dat woman needs to be helped into carriages, and lifted ober ditches, and to have de best place every whar. Nobody eber help me into carriages, or ober mud puddles, or gives me any best place and raising herself to her full height and her voice to a pitch like rolling thunder, she asked, *and ar'n't I a woman? Look at me! Look at my arm!* And she bared her right arm to the shoulder, showing her tremendous muscular power. *I have plowed, and planted, and gathered into barns, and no man could head me—and ar'n't I a woman? I could work as much and eat as much as a man (when I could get it), and bear de lash as well—*

*and ar'n't I a woman? I habe borne thirteen chilern and seen 'em mos'
all sold off into slavery, and when I cried out with a mother's grief,
none but Jesus heard—and ar'n't I a woman? Den dey talks 'bout
dis ting in de head—what dis dey call it?* "Intellect," whispered someone near. *Dat's it honey. What's dat got to do with women's rights
or niggers' rights? If my cup won't hold but a pint and yourn holds a
quart, wouldn't ye be mean not to let me have my little half-measure
full?* And she pointed her significant finger and sent a keen
glance at the minister who had made the argument. The cheering was long and loud.

*Den dat little man in black dar, he say women can't have as much
rights as man, cause Christ war'n't a woman. Whar did your Christ
come from?* Rolling thunder could not have stilled that crowd as
did those deep wonderful tones, as she stood there with out-
stretched arms and eye of fire. Raising her voice still louder, she
repeated, *Whar did your Christ come from? From God and a woman.
Man had nothing to do with him.* Oh! What a rebuke she gave the
little man.

Turning again to another objector, she took up the defense of
mother Eve. I cannot follow her through it all. It was pointed, and
witty, and solemn, eliciting at almost every sentence deafening
applause; and she ended by asserting that *if de fust woman God ever
made was strong enough to turn the world upside down, all 'lone, dese
togedder* and she glanced her eye over us, *ought to be able to turn it
back and get it right side up again, and now dey is asking to do it, de
men better let 'em.* Long-continued cheering. *Bleeged to ye for hearin'
on me, and now ole Sojourner ha'n't got nothing more to say.*

*Lord, I thank you for Sojourner Truth, for her courage and
honesty. I pray you would raise up many women with such a clean
spirit and honest heart—women who will advance your truth and
justice in this sad, hard world.*

RELATED SCRIPTURE READING—ACTS 16:11–15

MARY SLESSOR

(1848–1915)

My life is one long daily, hourly record of answered prayer. For physical health . . . for everything that goes to make up life and my poor service, I can testify with a full and often wonder-stricken awe that I believe God answers prayer.

I can give no other testimony. I am sitting alone here on a log among a company of natives. My children, whose very lives are a testimony that God answers prayer, are working round me. Natives are crowding past on the bush road to attend palavers [gatherings], and I am at perfect peace, far from my own countrymen and conditions, because I know God answers prayer. Food is scarce just now. . . . We have not more than will be our breakfast today, but I know we shall be fed, for God answers prayer.

FROM A LETTER BY MARY SLESSOR

Mary Slessor was the second of seven children of a shoemaker living in Dundee, Scotland. Sent to work in a mill, she spent half days at a school provided by the owners and half working as a weaver. By age fourteen Slessor worked twelve-hour days, yet her interest in religion led her to become a teacher at a nearby mission. Gospel work in the Dundee neighborhoods trained her to cope with physical and mental hardship.

In 1876 Slessor set sail as a missionary to the Nigerian region of Calabar. There the twenty-eight-year-old woman labored in a society torn apart by the slave trade. Witchcraft and superstition were common, human sacrifice routine, newborn twins ritually murdered, and women treated worse than cattle. Slessor encouraged trade, opposed slavery, and contributed greatly to the opening of Africa for the faith and for the commerce necessary to uplift the inhabitants' lives.

When Mary Slessor died, she was given a state funeral and her African grave was marked by a cross of Scottish granite. In 1953 Queen Elizabeth II visited the grave site.

Survival in the extreme conditions of Mary Slessor's work required that her prayers be answered. She had placed herself at the cutting edge of the advancing gospel and of the expanding influence of Western culture. Rarely if ever do Christians in America face such conditions. Usually our lives do not depend on our prayers because everything is in control. The food supply is secure. Health care is available. Our homes are warm and dry, and our communities are safe.

If this is the case, why pray?

The apostle Paul often mentions prayer but he doesn't usually tell the answers to his prayers. His most well-known prayer is found in 2 Corinthians 12:7–10. It is the one that was not answered as he wished.

He had a thorn in his flesh—a malady that he could not shake. He asked three times and yet God did not remove the thorn. Instead, God said to Paul, "My grace is sufficient for you, for power is made perfect in weakness" (v. 9). This is what most of us will gain from prayer—not the desired answers, but pointers to grace.

Philippians 4:6–7 may be Paul's most direct instruction on prayer. He says, "Do not worry about anything." Amazing! Instead, we are to make our requests known to God. This is simple. And what can we expect for answers? The apostle says, "The peace of God, which surpasses all understanding, will guard your hearts and your minds in Christ Jesus."

The reward of prayer is not specific answers. Although, as Mary Slessor testifies, this certainly does happen. Scripture says that what we get out of prayer is peace, guardian peace for our soul's passage through this life.

Father God, strengthen me to pray and sensitize my heart to recognize your answers to my prayers. Cause me to know that, as I daily pray, your mysterious peace is actively preserving my heart and mind in Christ.

RELATED SCRIPTURE READING—MATTHEW 26:39–46

ANTOINETTE BROWN
BLACKWELL

(1825–1921)

> This is a very poor and small church, and my salary is three hundred dollars a year, ample I believe for my needs in this small community. My parish will be a miniature world in good and evil. To get humanity condensed into so small a compass that I can study each individual, opens a new chapter of experience. It is what I want, although it rolls upon the spirit a burden of deep responsibility. Perhaps I shall know some of the feelings with which an Infinite Mind watches the universe.
>
> FROM *ANTOINETTE BROWN BLACKWELL: A BIOGRAPHY*

The first American woman ordained as a minister was born in Henrietta, New York. Antoinette Louisa Brown attended Oberlin College in Ohio, the first coeducational college to grant degrees to women and to accept students of all races.

Graduated in 1847, Brown decided to study theology. The college did not think this an appropriate field of study for a woman. But Brown prevailed because the school's charter stated that no student could be excluded on the basis of sex. She finished the theology course in 1850, but Oberlin refused to award her the degree and she could not receive a license to preach. (Twenty-eight years later the college conferred her degree.)

Following the completion of her theological training, Brown traveled the lecture circuit, speaking in favor of the abolition of slavery and the prohibition of alcohol consumption.

On the recommendation of Horace Greeley, on September 15, 1853, Brown was ordained a minister of the First Congregational Church in South Butler, New York, but in 1854 she withdrew from the congregation due to theological differences and took her ministry to the slums and prisons of New York City.

She married Samuel Blackwell in 1856. While Antoinette Blackwell cared for her family of five daughters, she worked as a writer. In *The Sexes Throughout Nature* (1875), she asserts that Darwin failed to understand the roles of the sexes. Altogether, ten of her books were published.

What lesson can be drawn from this remarkable woman's life? Her words about the work in New York City give a hint:

> We went wherever the way seemed prepared for rescue work
> . . . perhaps to the Hospital, the workhouse, the Insane Asylum,
> or the Penitentiary on Blackwell's Island with some message of
> good will or moral tonic.

"We went wherever the way seemed prepared." This sound rule has a source in Scripture. On his second journey the apostle Paul traveled through the land that is present-day Turkey (Acts 15:36–41). In Lystra Timothy joined him and Silas, and they trekked northwestward toward the Roman province of Asia. But the Book of Acts records, they were "forbidden by the Holy Spirit to speak the word in Asia" (16:6).

They did no gospel work in Asia. Instead, the party traveled due north. "They attempted to go into Bithynia, but the Spirit of Jesus did not allow them" (v. 7). So they went west to Troas.

They traveled about five hundred miles on foot before arriving at a place where they could minister. This journey can be explained with Antoinette Blackwell's words: "We went wherever the way seemed prepared." The way *was* prepared for Paul— not to Asia, not to Bithynia, but directly to Europe, where the gospel gained a foothold in the city of Philippi in present-day Greece (vv. 11–12). The apostle did not force the gospel into Asia or Bithynia. Instead, the Spirit opened a fertile path for him, he followed it, and the truth blossomed beautifully in Greece.

Dearest Holy Spirit, I would like to follow you more closely.
Sensitize my heart to your impulses so that I may know the peace of
traveling on the ways you open.

RELATED SCRIPTURE READING—JOHN 4:1–6

AIMEE SEMPLE MCPHERSON

(1890–1944)

You all remember, perhaps, the story of a little girl who some
time ago discovered a broken rail on a certain railroad track. She
had wits enough about her to run to a telephone and call the
superintendent, or rather I should say, the man at the depot.
And he said, "Little girl, the train's already passed the station
. . . stop it some way!" She never thought to argue. She said, "I'm
little, but I'll do my best." She ran so fast and she waved her
apron so hard, that the train stopped, and every life was saved.

This is my task.

It isn't how important you are and what great knowledge you
have—it's a willingness to do it. To let God fill your life. Amen!

ANGELUS TEMPLE, LOS ANGELES, MARCH 12, 1939

Aimee Semple McPherson was one of America's most flam-
boyant revivalists. Born in Salford, Ontario, the daughter of
farmers, she served briefly as a missionary to Hong Kong, was a
national sensation as a preacher, and founded the International
Church of the Foursquare Gospel.

In 1907 Aimee Elizabeth Kennedy married the Pentecostal
preacher who had led her to the Christian faith, Robert Semple. They traveled to China as missionaries, but both were soon
hospitalized with malaria and dysentery. In August 1910 Robert
died. A month later Aimee gave birth to a baby girl. Aimee
returned to the United States and joined her mother in New
York. There in 1912 she married Harold McPherson.

Known to her followers as Sister Aimee, McPherson pio-
neered radio evangelism, beginning to broadcast in 1922.
McPherson's teaching consisted of standard fundamentalist and
Pentecostal emphases: sanctification, baptism of the Holy Spirit
with the gift of tongues, Christ as Savior and healer, and the
imminent return of Christ.

After World War I, Aimee Semple McPherson traveled with her mother on a successful series of revival tours across the United States. On one side of her automobile was painted "JESUS IS COMING SOON—GET READY." On the other side was the question, "WHERE WILL YOU SPEND ETERNITY?" McPherson called this the "Gospel Car." She and her mother are thought to be the first women to successfully travel in an automobile across the continental United States.

In 1922 she settled in Los Angeles, where she preached to thousands each week at her 1.5-million-dollar Angelus Temple. She introduced jazz music into the church and popularized the use of stage plays to dramatize sermons.

The gifted and articulate Aimee Semple McPherson had a natural exuberance and a powerful presence. She called her message the Gospel of Reconciliation and Love. By this she meant that God loves humanity, desires the very best for each person, and has provided a way for each one to find divine peace through Jesus Christ.

McPherson easily attracted controversy because she was an attractive woman with a style and personality that were entirely different from those of other preachers. But considering her work in retrospect, we must agree with the apostle Paul, "What does it matter? Just this, that Christ is proclaimed in every way, . . . and in that I rejoice. Yes, and I will continue to rejoice" (Philippians 1:18).

Lord, I love you, and I love your gospel of salvation. Thank you that its truth found a way into my heart. May people's hearts open to your sweet love and relax in you.

RELATED SCRIPTURE READING—GALATIANS 2:7–10

AMY CARMICHAEL

(1867–1951)

Hast thou no scar?
No hidden scar on foot, or side, or hand?
I hear thee sung as mighty in the land,
I hear them hail thy bright, ascendant star,
Hast thou no scar?

Hast thou no wound?
Yet I was wounded by the archers, spent,
Leaned Me against a tree to die; and rent
By ravening beasts that compassed Me, I swooned:
Hast thou no wound?

No wound? No scar?
Yes, as the Master shall the servant be,
And pierced are the feet that follow Me;
But thine are whole: can he have followed far
Who has no wound nor scar?

AMY CARMICHAEL, "TOWARD JERUSALEM"

Amy Carmichael grew up in a prominent family in Northern Ireland. When she was eighteen, her father died, and financial pressures caused the family to move to Belfast. There Carmichael became involved in city mission work. A desire to serve God as a missionary arose in her, and at age twenty-six she went to Japan. Unable to continue her work there because of poor health and the Japanese climate, she went without the approval of her mission board to Ceylon. Carmichael eventually arrived in Tamil Nadu, thirty miles from the southern tip of India. This was her home for the next fifty-five years, where her life's work was that of rescuing children from Hindu temple prostitution. Carmichael founded Dohnavur Fellowship and rescued, raised, and educated hundreds of children. A serious fall in 1931 left her an invalid for the final twenty years of her life.

In giving her life to the children of India, Carmichael exemplifies Christ's call for us to forsake all and follow him. He who died for us asks us to follow in his steps.

The Gospel of John tells of Jesus riding a donkey into Jerusalem and the crowds shouting praises and covering the road he traveled with their coats and with leaves from the trees (12:12–15). Jesus was suddenly fashionable. People wanted to crown him as their king. He responded, "Unless a grain of wheat falls into the earth and dies, it remains just a single grain; but if it dies, it bears much fruit" (v. 24). He did not come to Jerusalem that day as a national hero; he came as the Savior to die the death that would redeem all creation to God.

"Whoever serves me must follow me," he told them that day (v. 26). Given their exuberance, many people would have followed. But before the week was out, the exultant crowds were gone, and Jesus, beaten bloody, was dead.

Here is what it means to follow Christ: "Do you not know," asks Paul, "that all of us who have been baptized into Christ Jesus were baptized into his death?" (Romans 6:3). Or, as Amy Carmichael wrote, "Can he have followed far / Who has no wound nor scar?"

The Christian gospel is about a death—the planting of a single grain of wheat named Jesus Christ. He is now bringing forth an abundant harvest of eternal life in resurrection. Paul continues, "Therefore we have been buried with him by baptism into death, so that, just as Christ was raised from the dead by the glory of the Father, so we too might walk in newness of life" (v. 4).

Lord Jesus Christ, thank you that by baptism I have been united with you in your death, and I trust that I will be united with you in resurrection.

RELATED SCRIPTURE READING—1 CORINTHIANS 15:35–37, 42–45

GLADYS AYLWARD

(1904–1970)

England, seemingly so prosperous while other countries passed through terrible suffering at the hands of Communist domination, had forgotten what was all-important—the realization that God mattered in the life of a nation no less than in that of an individual.

From a letter by Gladys Aylward

Gladys Aylward was the daughter of a London postman. While she was working as a domestic servant, Aylward responded to a revival sermon and dedicated her life to God. She felt called to preach the gospel in China but failed the examination for missionary service. Not deterred, she saved her money to pay her own way to China.

In 1932 Aylward set out on the Trans-Siberian Railway—a perilous journey via Vladivostok to Tientsin, China. From there she found her way to the mountainous province of Shansi and the inland city of Yangcheng, south of Beijing. There she joined missionary Jeannie Lawson, age seventy-three, and they set up an inn to bring the gospel to the passing mule train drivers. The men were given food and lodging plus free entertainment—stories about Jesus Christ. Many of the lodgers remembered these stories and retold them as they traveled. Some became believers.

Aylward's story is truly remarkable. She lived frugally, dressed like the common people, and was a welcome visitor at the mandarin's (governor's) palace. In 1936 she became a Chinese citizen.

In the spring of 1938, the Japanese bombed Yangcheng, and the Japanese Army began a series of intermittent occupations of the city. Aylward helped find shelter for the refugees, and as the war continued, often gave aid and military intelligence to the Chinese armies. The Japanese offered a bounty for her capture, so she fled by foot with nearly one hundred orphans. After an epic exodus of one hundred hazardous miles lasting nearly a month, Aylward and the orphans arrived at Sian, where Aylward collapsed with typhus, pneumonia, and exhaustion. As a result, Aylward's health was permanently damaged and in 1947 she returned to England for medical care.

Gladys Aylward was truly a light in the world. Her life reflected this prayer in Ephesians 1: "that with the eyes of your heart enlightened, you may know what is the hope to which he has called you, and what is the immeasurable greatness of his power for us who believe" (vv. 18–19).

In 1957 Alan Burgess wrote a book about Aylward, *The Small Woman*. This was condensed in *Reader's Digest* and was the basis of the Hollywood movie *The Inn of the Sixth Happiness*, starring Ingrid Bergman, which was loosely based on Aylward's life.

The Communist takeover of China forced Gladys Aylward and other missionaries to leave their work while the Christian faith was suppressed among the native Chinese. Yet the church survived there to enjoy dramatic growth. It is estimated that between the Communist takeover in 1949 and the mid-1980s, the church in China grew from 800,000 to as many as 50 million—one of the greatest surges of growth in church history. This is in part a testimony to the solid foundation built by Aylward and the thousands of missionaries who for a century labored among the Chinese people.

At the end of her life Aylward wrote: "My heart is full of praise that one so insignificant, uneducated, and ordinary in every way could be used to His glory for the blessing of His people in poor persecuted China."

Dear Father of glory, give me a spirit of wisdom and revelation so that I may know you. Enlighten the eyes of my heart so I may know the hope to which I am called and the riches of your glorious inheritance among the saints.

RELATED SCRIPTURE READING—MATTHEW 25:1–13

41

PART 3

THE WIVES
AND
MOTHERS

AUGUSTINE'S MOTHER, MONICA

(331–387)

By this time my mother had come to me. . . . She found me in deadly peril through my despair of ever finding the truth. But when I told her that I was now no longer a Manichean, though not yet a [true] Christian, she did not leap for joy as if this were unexpected. . . . Instead, she was fully confident that you who had promised the whole would give her the rest, and . . . she replied to me that she believed, in Christ, that before she died she would see me a faithful [Christian]. And she said no more than this to me. But to you, O fountain of mercy, she poured out still more frequent prayers and tears that you would hasten your aid and enlighten my darkness, . . . praying for the fountain of water that springs up into everlasting life.

FROM *CONFESSIONS* BY AUGUSTINE

Monica was born into a Christian family at Tagaste, North Africa, about 150 miles from Carthage. All that is known of her is told by her son Augustine in his autobiographical book *Confessions*.

Monica's firstborn was Augustine, born in 354. She later gave birth to another son, Naviguus, and a daughter whose name is unknown. Patricius, her irritable husband, was eventually won over to Christ by Monica's patience.

When Augustine came of age, he moved about the Roman Empire, and Monica joined him in Milan where the young man was attracted to the preaching of Ambrose. At last converted, he was baptized on Easter, 387. The same year, while returning to Africa, Monica died at age fifty-six.

Augustine attested that, because of his mother's testimony and prayer, God "drew his soul out of the profound darkness." He prayed to God, "She saw that I was dead by that faith and spirit which she had from you, and you heard her, O Lord."

Monica is the original and chief example of service to God through motherhood. The testimony of her life and her prayer preserved and prepared her son Augustine for the church. He was among the foremost theologians of early Christianity and he profoundly influenced the development of Western thought and culture. His work to unify the theology of the early church allowed Christianity to become the religion of medieval Europe, and his thought has remained basic to Western Christianity, both Roman Catholic and Protestant, to this day.

The Christian faith, he claimed, is not external and visible. Augustine insisted that Christianity was a matter of the spirit within a believer, not obedience to external laws. Plus, he said that the church includes sinners *and* saints. Those members who seem to be holy and blessed must not exclude those whom God, through grace, is perfecting.

Confessions records Monica's words to her son before she died:

> There was indeed one thing for which I wished to tarry a little in this life, and that was that I might see you a Christian before I died. My God has exceeded this abundantly. . . .

After Monica's death, Augustine returned to North Africa where the church was struggling under heretical influences. In 396 he became bishop of Hippo.

As the Empire fell, in 430 Hippo came under military siege. In the midst of ministering to refugees, Augustine contracted a fatal disease and died.

Augustine's *Confessions* paints a clear picture of a life under the transforming power of the Christian gospel. An emotionally moving book, it testifies of Christ's work in this great man— a work initiated by his mother's prayer.

Lord, reach the hearts of mothers and fathers everywhere and become their wisdom in raising children. Let their prayer and endurance bring forth new leaders, thinkers, and workers to meet the extraordinary spiritual need of this world and your church.

RELATED SCRIPTURE READING—2 TIMOTHY 1:3–5

HELOISE

(CA. 1098–1164)

And so in His Name to whom you have offered yourself, before God I beseech you that in whatsoever way you can, you restore to me your presence, to wit by writing me some word of comfort. To this end alone that, thus refreshed, I may give myself with more willingness to the service of God. . . . Consider, I beseech you, what you owe me, pay heed to what I demand; and my long letter with a brief ending I conclude. Farewell, my all.

FROM HELOISE'S FIRST LETTER TO ABELARD

The learned Frenchwoman Heloise was the niece of Fulbert, the bishop of Chartres. When Heloise was eighteen years old, her tutor was Peter Abelard, whose thought influenced many of the religious minds of the twelfth century. He is considered the first modern thinker and the most brilliant man of his time.

Abelard and Heloise are classic figures among the world's lovers. The couple was secretly married and Heloise had a son by Abelard. But Fulbert, outraged by the relationship, had Abelard emasculated and disgraced. Their child, Astrolabe, was left to be raised without his parents. The couple did not see one another again for ten years.

Heloise became a monastic and entered the Convent of St. Argenteuil near Paris. In 1129 she became superior of the Benedictine Abbey of the Paraclete (which had been built by Abelard). Abelard spent his final days in a monastery in Cluny. Heloise died twenty-two years after her husband and was buried next to his grave in the Paraclete in Troyes.

The letters of Abelard and Heloise are among the best-known documents of early romantic love. Abelard and Heloise deserve to be called the creators of the modern ideal of marriage. Though they never had the opportunity to live together as husband and wife, they voluntarily shared tenderness, support, and shelter from the world.

Abelard and Heloise were contemporaries of the first troubadours in the early days of courtly love. No wonder Heloise's first letter to Abelard begins with this lush salutation: "To her master, nay father, to her husband, nay brother; his handmaid, nay daughter, his spouse, nay sister: To Abelard, Heloise."

The marriage of Heloise and Abelard occurred at the time when marriage was quickly becoming incompatible with a church career; their unrestrained expressions of love, though reminders of the words of the Bible, quickly fell out of fashion. But the Bible remained to tell of love in luxuriant language, like this fragment of the Song of Solomon: "I slept, but my heart was awake. Listen! my beloved is knocking. 'Open to me, my sister, my love, my dove, my perfect one; for my head is wet with dew, my locks with the drops of the night'" (5:2).

Bible teachers have been embarrassed by the words of this book. In fact the early rabbis would not allow young men to read the Song lest it inflame their imagination. The book has its source in ancient Middle Eastern marriage songs. Now it is interpreted as the description of the love between God and a believer, or of Christ and the church.

If so, then it must also describe the love of an everyday man and woman. Why? Because Ephesians compares married love with the divine: "Husbands, love your wives, just as Christ loved the church and gave himself up for her" (5:25). Any man who can say to his wife, "You have ravished my heart, my sister, my bride . . . with a glance of your eyes, with one jewel of your necklace. How sweet is your love, my sister, my bride! how much better is your love than wine, and the fragrance of your oils than any spice!" (Song 4:9–10) has surely given himself up for her.

Dear Lord, inflame my heart with true love for my spouse. Teach me selflessness in my relationships. Please let my life, in some small way, reflect the love you have for the church and for all humanity.

RELATED SCRIPTURE READING—SONG OF SOLOMON 7:1–9

KATHERINE VON BORA LUTHER

(1499–1552)

Who would not be sorrowful and mourn for so noble a man as my dear lord, who served not only a single land, but the whole world? If I had a principality and an empire, it would never have cost me so much pain to lose them as I have now that our dear Lord God has taken from me, and not from me only, but from the whole world, this dear and precious man.

FROM A LETTER BY KATHERINE VON BORA LUTHER

It is said that Martin Luther did not seriously consider marriage because he thought he would one day be burned at the stake, leaving a wife as a widow. But Katherine Von Bora married him in 1525. She was twenty-six; he was forty-two.

Von Bora was born of a noble family in Saxony. When her mother died and her father remarried, Katherine was sent to a Cistercian cloister where an aunt was the abbess and many of the residents were from noble families. Katherine became a nun in 1515.

At that time Martin Luther was an Augustinian monk lecturing on the Bible at the University of Wittenberg. In 1517 he issued his famous Ninety-five Theses against indulgences in the Roman Catholic Church and the tumultuous Reformation began. Soon monks and nuns were seeking freedom from convents and monasteries.

Shortly before Easter, 1523, a merchant made a delivery to Von Bora's convent. She and others hid in the merchant's wagon and were taken to New Saxony, an area sympathetic toward Luther and his views. From there they continued to Wittenberg where Luther found housing for them.

Biographers say that Luther and Von Bora had a happy marriage. They lived in a former Augustinian convent with their six children and cared for various nieces and nephews. Visitors were welcomed. Tutors and students from the university stayed in their home. During the meals, these young scholars took notes on Luther's discussions—now published in volumes titled *Table Talk*.

At the time of Martin Luther and Katherine Von Bora's marriage, the familial bond had lost the respect of society. Marriage and children were objects of scorn, and women were often subjected to open hostility. Similarly today, many are rejecting marriage and children. In the United States the marital bond is under attack, there is some repugnance for traditional feminine roles, and fatherhood is belittled; the entertainment industry celebrates fornication, and the federal tax code rewards cohabitation.

The pre-Reformation church said that marriage was a channel of God's sanctifying grace, but in practice the church gave a celibate priest, monk, or nun higher status than a married person. Though most priests, monks, and nuns labored faithfully, some turned to debauchery. Luther noted that marriage had fallen universally into "awful disrepute." By abolishing the practice of priestly celibacy and monasticism, the Reformation gave marriage and family a new place of sanctity in Europe.

Father, teach each husband to love his wife as himself and each wife to respect her husband. Somehow, dear God, strengthen marriage and family just as you did in the days of Katherine and Martin Luther.

RELATED SCRIPTURE READING—EPHESIANS 5:25–33

SUSANNA WESLEY

(1669–1742)

Consider well what a separation from the world, what purity, what devotion, what exemplary virtue, are required in those who are to guide others to glory. . . . Begin and end the day with him who is the Alpha and Omega, and if you really experience what it is to love God, you will redeem all the time you can for his more immediate service.

Endeavor to act upon principle and do not live like the rest of mankind, who pass through the world like straws upon a river, which are carried which way the stream or wind drive them. . . . Get as deep an impression on your mind as is possible of the constant presence of the great and holy God. He is about our beds and about our paths and spies out all our ways. Whenever you are tempted to the commission of any sin, or the omission of any duty, pause and say to yourself, "What am I about to do? God sees me."

WRITTEN BY SUSANNA WESLEY TO HER ELDEST SON, SAMUEL

Born the youngest daughter of twenty-five children to a family of comfortable social standing, Susanna Annesley was well educated by her father, a clergyman. In 1688, at age nineteen, she married Samuel Wesley, seven years her senior. Samuel Wesley was rector for forty years at the remote English village of Epworth. The couple had nineteen children. Of the nine who lived to maturity, the best known is John, the founder of Methodism.

The Wesley home in Epworth burned twice. The second fire, in 1709, trapped John, age five, in the nursery. He had the presence of mind to push a chest to the window and stand on it to be seen by rescuers and brought to safety. Susanna thereafter called John "a brand plucked from the burning," and in her journal wrote, "I do intend to be more particularly careful of the soul of this child."

Susanna was twenty-one years old when she gave birth to her first child and around forty when her last was born. In her first twenty years of marriage, not a year passed that she did not either begin or end a pregnancy.

Her husband, Samuel, was a learned man and strongly principled but a poor money manager. He once spent a year in jail for nonpayment of bills. Susanna was left with the responsibility for the household. Still, she sent Samuel her only jewelry—a wedding band—to assure that he had food. Her journal records: "I have learned, from the best observations I have been able to make . . . that it is much easier to be contented without riches than if with them."

Formal education for the Wesley children began at age five. Susanna Wesley taught her various children for six hours daily for twenty years. The curriculum included Latin, Greek, French, and logic. She did not teach her children practical skills until each could read well. An amazing woman!

When Samuel was absent from Epworth, Susanna gathered her household on Sunday evenings to sing psalms, listen to the reading of sermons, and read the *Book of Common Prayer*. The group included neighbors and steadily grew in number. Eventually Susanna held a complete Anglican service in her kitchen. Also she set aside one hour in the morning and one in the evening for personal meditation and prayer—a practice she learned from her father.

Although modern life is entirely different from Wesley's eighteenth century, we share in common with her the love and worship of God. Then as now God is seeking true worshipers like Susanna Wesley, people who will worship the Father in spirit and truth (John 4:23–24).

O Father of the Lord Jesus Christ, give me a spirit of wisdom and revelation as I come to know you. Enlighten the eyes of my heart that I may know what is the hope to which you have called me and what are the riches of your glorious inheritance among the saints.

RELATED SCRIPTURE READING—EPHESIANS 1:15–21

51

SUSANNA WESLEY

A PRAYER

I give you praise, O God, for a well-spent day. But I am yet unsatisfied, because I do not enjoy enough of you. I would have my soul more closely united to you by faith and love. I would love you above all things. You, who has made me, know my desires, my expectations. My joys all center in you and it is you yourself that I desire; it is your favor, your acceptance, the communications of your grace that I earnestly wish for, more than anything in the world.

FROM SUSANNA WESLEY'S DIARY

Susanna Wesley was the daughter of Dr. Samuel Annesley, a well-known Noncomformist minister who held his doctorate from Oxford. He preached before the British House of Commons and served parishes at St. Giles, Cripplegate, and London.

Of Susanna and Samuel Wesley's nineteen children, only nine lived to adulthood. At their home in Epworth (eastern England), Susanna was her children's educator and wrote two textbooks for them: *A Manual of Natural Theory* and *An Exposition of the Leading Truths of the Gospel*. A third book was written specifically for her daughter Emilia.

It is said that Samuel once asked Susanna in exasperation, "Why do you sit there teaching that dull child that lesson over the twentieth time?" She replied, "Had I satisfied myself by mentioning the matter only nineteen times, I should have lost all labor. You see it was the twentieth time that crowned the whole."

When her son John, the founder of Methodism, asked her to write some details of her method of education of her children, Susanna consented but confessed, "No one can, without renouncing the world in the most literal sense, observe my method. There are few, if any, who would devote about twenty years of the prime of life in hopes to save the souls of their children."

Another son, Charles, wrote some eight thousand hymns—an average of three per week for fifty-three years. These compositions include "Hark! the Herald Angels Sing," "Christ the Lord Is Risen Today," and "O for a Thousand Tongues to Sing." He was steeped in the best of the literature in English, Latin, and Greek, associated this literature with Scripture, and produced amazing lyrics for hymns still important to the church for worship and teaching. One of the less well-known of Charles Wesley's hymns is "Our Hearts Are Full of Christ"—two verses set to an old English melody. Here is the second verse of this hymn:

> Fairer than all the earthborn race,
> Perfect in comeliness thou are;
> Replenished are thy lips with grace,
> And full of love thy tender heart.
> God ever-blest! We bow the knee,
> And own all fullness dwells in thee.

This beautiful word sketch stirs one's desire to enjoy God. Like the psalmist sang: "As a deer longs for flowing streams, so my soul longs for you, O God. My soul thirsts for God, for the living God" (Psalm 42:1–2). This ancient impulse to enjoy the Lord was expressed in part through the Shorter Westminster Catechism, which may be the very source of Susanna Wesley's desire for such pleasure. Composed of 107 questions and answers, the Catechism is a brief introduction to the rule and essence of the Christian religion. The first question and answer are well-known and provide information that can bring joy and satisfaction to each day of a believer's life:

Question 1: What is the chief end of man?
Answer: To glorify God, and to enjoy him forever.

Heavenly Father, my joys all center in you and it is you yourself that I desire; it is your favor, your acceptance, the communications of your grace that I earnestly wish for, more than anything in the world.

RELATED SCRIPTURE READING—PHILIPPIANS 4:4–7

ANN JUDSON

(1789–1826)

> I am a creature of God, and he has an undoubted right to do with me as seems good in his sight. I rejoice that I am in his hand—that he is everywhere present and can protect me in one place as well as in another. . . . Whether I spend my days in India or America, I desire to spend them in the service of God, and be prepared to spend an eternity in his presence. . . . I am quite willing to give up temporal comforts and live a life of hardship and trial, if it be the will of God. . . . "Behold the handmaid of the Lord; be it unto me according to thy word" (Luke 1:38).
>
> FROM ANN JUDSON'S JOURNAL

Ann Judson and her husband, Adoniram, were the first American missionaries to establish work in Far Eastern Asia. Ann Hasseltine was a schoolteacher when she met Judson, a Congregational minister. Within a few days of their marriage in 1812, the couple departed for missionary work in India. During the voyage, they studied about baptism in preparation to meet British Baptists in India and, as a result, embraced the Baptist view.

The Judsons soon went to Rangoon, Burma, and began to study the native language, in which they found no words for God, heaven, or eternity. In 1815 Ann Judson gave birth to a son, the first child born of white parents in Burma. He died eight months later. She then worked at translating the Bible into Burmese and opened a school for girls. Weakened by tropical illnesses, Ann Judson returned to America in 1822.

She came back to the field of her labor as war broke out between Burma and Britain. Adoniram was imprisoned and, were it not for the daily efforts of his wife, would have died in prison. During her husband's confinement, Ann gave birth to a daughter. When the war was over, the couple moved to Amherst in lower Burma. While Adoniram was away, Ann contracted a fever and died at age thirty-seven. Their daughter died six months later.

Ann Judson is the foremost missionary heroine of the American people. She stands as eloquent proof that sacred service includes the ministration of a wife to her husband. "Therefore a man leaves his father and his mother and clings to his wife, and they become one flesh" (Genesis 2:24).

Adoniram Judson doubtless clung to his wife. When Judson was arrested and carried off to a death prison, Ann, awaiting the birth of their second child, was placed under house arrest. Yet she managed to send necessities to her husband and other prisoners. He was secretly moved to another prison, so with babe in arms and two adopted children, Ann set off to find him. She eventually did so; he was chained to other prisoners in a stifling building.

While she struggled for her husband, Ann herself was stricken with disease, and exhausted. Finally, Adoniram was imprisoned where she could not locate him. Then she wrote in a letter:

> If I ever felt the value of efficacy of prayer, I did at this time. . . . I could make no efforts to secure my husband. I could only plead with that great and powerful being who has said, "Call upon me in the day of trouble and I will hear. . . ." God made me at this time feel so powerfully this promise that I became quite composed, feeling assured that my prayers would be answered.

After the deaths of his wife and daughter, Adoniram Judson wrote to Ann's mother: "We made the child's last bed in the small enclosure that surrounded her mother's lonely grave. Together they rest in hope, under the hope tree, which stands at the head of the graves. . . . And I am left alone in the wide world."

Dearest Lord, hear my prayer for husbands that they would love their wives as they do their own bodies. Let men know, O God, that he who loves his wife loves himself. Let the man nourish and tenderly care for the woman, just as Christ does the church.

RELATED SCRIPTURE READING—EPHESIANS 5:25–33

MARY MOFFAT LIVINGSTONE

(1820–1862)

And now, my dearest, farewell. Let your affection be towards
[Christ] much more than towards me: and kept by his mighty power
and grace, I hope I shall never give you cause to regret that you
have given me a part. Whatever friendship we feel towards each
other, let us always look at Jesus as our common friend and guide,
and may he shield you with his everlasting arms from every evil.

DAVID LIVINGSTONE IN A LETTER TO HIS WIFE

Mary Moffat was born at Griquatown in southern Africa, firstborn of the British missionaries Mary and Robert Moffat. In 1840
her future husband was brought to Africa by Mary's father's stir-
ring words about "the smoke of a thousand villages" where no
missionary had been. David Livingstone met Mary Moffat when
she was twenty-three years old. They married in 1845 and Mary
embarked on a life of suffering for the sake of the gospel.

After moving about southern Africa, the Livingstones made
their home at Kolobeng (the name means "haunt of the wild
boar"). Mary's life was not unlike that of other pioneer women
of the time: perils in travel, incessant work, sickness, deaths of
children, threats from native inhabitants, and the like. Mary
was more than once plagued with partial paralysis brought on
by disease. At one point she and her six children returned to
England for four years so that she could regain her health. There
she lived in near poverty.

Meanwhile David made his famous four-year epochal journey in central Africa. He brought the gospel to the region, made
inroads against the slave trade, and made important contribu-
tions to zoology, paleontology, geography, geology, climatology,
and astronomy. Though he always expressed great love for his
wife, his work was incompatible with the duties of a father and
husband. He returned to England a hero in 1856.

At Mary's death, Livingstone wrote in his journal: "Oh my Mary, my Mary! How often we have longed for a quiet home since you and I were cast adrift at Kolobeng . . . [the Father] has rewarded you by taking you to a better home, the eternal one in the heavens."

Is there a sacrifice that is too great to give for the sake of the gospel? Martyrs like Anne Askew and Mary Dyer thought not and gave their lives. Missionaries by the thousands have given up all they had to bring the message of God's love to distant people. As David Livingstone and his family set off in ox-drawn wagons for the remote Zambesi River, he wrote:

> It is a venture to take wife and children into a country where fever—African fever—prevails. But who that believes in Jesus would refuse to make a venture for such a Captain? . . . May he bless us and make us blessings even unto death.

Most Christians in America may never have an opportunity to be like Paul and Barnabas and Mary Livingstone, and countless others "who have risked their lives for the sake of our Lord Jesus Christ" (Acts 15:26). But today there are reports from faraway places that the persecution of Christians is increasing. There are women like Mary Livingstone living at this moment who are in need of prayer and practical support, women at risk who would despair for life without the succor of the church.

The gospel takes account of our response to such suffering: "Come, you that are blessed by my Father, inherit the kingdom prepared for you from the foundation of the world; for I was hungry and you gave me food, . . . I was a stranger and you welcomed me" (Matthew 25:34–35).

Dear God, soften my heart to the needs of people who suffer simply because they are Christians. I pray that their stories be told throughout the world and that relief will reach those who love you.

RELATED SCRIPTURE READING—LUKE 10:29–37

MARIA DYER TAYLOR

(CA. 1840–1870)

All at once I became conscious of dear Maria's presence. She came in silently as a breath of air, and I felt such a tranquillity steal over me—I knew she must be there. I felt spellbound for a short time, but at length without opening my eyes, I put out my hand, and she took it in a warm, soft grasp. She motioned me not to speak, and put her other hand on my forehead, and I felt the headache and the fever retire under its touch and sink as through the pillow. She whispered to me not to be uneasy, that she was mine and I was hers, and that I must keep quiet and try to sleep. And so I did, awaking some hours later well of the fever though very weak.

A sweet dream, I would call it; only I was as wide awake as I am now, and saw and felt her touch as plainly as I do now pencil and paper. All my fear in the fever had been that our love would come to nothing, so you may guess how it soothed me.

FROM A LETTER BY HUDSON TAYLOR

An orphan, Maria Dyer was raised by her uncle in London. While still in her teen years, she entered the mission field as a teacher in Ningpo, China. There she met and married the young missionary, James Hudson Taylor, who would soon found the China Inland Mission. "She was spiritually minded, as her work proved," Taylor said; ". . . she was a true missionary."

This statement is from the man who is the archetype of the ideal worker for God. Called to the work in China in 1849, Hudson Taylor prepared by studying medicine, theology, and biblical languages. He practiced complete dependence on God for his material needs; he adopted native Chinese dress, a scandal at the time; he evangelized the interior provinces of China where no European had ever been before; he was one of the most profound spiritual influences in the history of modern China.

In the twelfth year of the Taylor marriage, in the midst of an outbreak of cholera, Maria gave birth to her sixth child, the fifth boy. He died of cholera within a week. "And now farewell, precious friend," she wrote. "The Lord throw around you his everlasting arms." A short time later, Maria Taylor died of the same disease and was embraced by those very same everlasting arms.

Scripture mentions people like Maria Taylor, "who through faith conquered kingdoms, administered justice, obtained promises, shut the mouths of lions, . . . of whom the world was not worthy" (Hebrews 11:33, 38). The rest of us must bow in thanksgiving to God for such lives.

After the death of his wife and son, Hudson Taylor wrote:

> How lonesome were the weary hours when confined to my room. How I missed my dear wife and the little pattering footsteps of the children far away in England! Then it was I understood why the Lord had made that passage so real to me, "Whosoever drinketh of the water that I shall give him shall never thirst." Twenty times a day, perhaps, as I felt the heart-thirst coming back, I cried to him: "Lord, you promised! You promised me that I should never thirst." And whether I called by day or night, how quickly he always came and satisfied my sorrowing heart!
>
> FROM THE *BIOGRAPHY OF JAMES HUDSON TAYLOR*

It was 140 years ago that Maria and Hudson Taylor lived in China and delivered the good news of Jesus Christ to the people there. Yet the quality of their lives speaks to twenty-first-century hearts—your heart and mine. As if addressing us directly, the apostle Paul advises, "But as for you, continue in what you have learned and firmly believed, knowing from whom you learned it" (2 Timothy 3:14). We have learned true commitment from Maria Dyer Taylor and a myriad of others whose lives testify to the veracity of the gospel of Jesus Christ and allow no doubt of its effectiveness in human life.

Thank you, Lord, for the cloud of witnesses that surrounds me. Let me lay aside every weight and the sin that clings so closely so I may, like them, run with perseverance the race that is set before me.

RELATED SCRIPTURE READING—HEBREWS 12:1–7

MARY MOFFAT

(1795-1870)

The willow tree is majestic; the syringas have been one sheet of blooms, and the perfume delicious, and now the orange trees are sending forth their still more grateful scent. The pomegranate hedge, with its numerous scarlet flowers, exceeds everything. The grass is again growing, and all nature looks gay at Kuruman.

FROM A LETTER BY MARY MOFFAT

The life of Mary Moffat was not unlike those Paul commends in Romans 16. It displayed the gospel in action and the fruit of the truth. Romans 16 is a wonderful note of greetings, recommendations, and appreciation for members of the faith community. Without this record of sweet relationships in Christ would the Book of Romans be the exquisite archive of first-century faith, which we know it to be? Certainly it would still be the clear, seamless account of the gospel of God. But unless this gospel is displayed in real life, in human relationships, it remains a myth, or at best, a philosophy. Therefore Romans 16 mentions thirty-eight individuals (including Jesus Christ)—plus one, the apostle Paul himself, whose service to God was exemplary.

It is not simply a list of church members; it is a testament to people's actions and interrelationships: Phoebe was a benefactor of many. Prisca and Aquila were Paul's coworkers; the church was in their house. Epaenetus was the first fruit of the gospel in Asia. Mary worked very hard among the believers.

The chronicle continues. There are relatives, saints, and entire churches. Even Paul's secretary, Tertius, is here (v. 22). The entire book of Romans becomes more precious when its potent phrases come alive in the citizens of the community of faith.

To Mary Moffat the gospel transcended teaching, doctrine, and method. Her decades of labor in South Africa caused the gospel to come alive in the hearts of Africans. The truth was made visible in the believers of Kuruman, southern Africa.

Born in New Windsor, England, Mary Smith traveled to Cape Town, South Africa, to marry missionary Robert Moffat in 1819. The couple eventually settled at Kuruman, six hundred miles from Cape Town in present-day Botswana. Mary kept house in extremely primitive conditions, washing in a river and producing necessities out of materials at hand. In time the Moffats established a prosperous mission station.

In the early years they despaired. "Could we but see the smallest fruit, we could rejoice midst the privations and toils we bear," Mary wrote in a letter home. "But as it is, our hands do often hang down." Later, however, she wrote to her family, "The longer we live in this land, the more convinced we are of the necessity of missionaries being here, being fully persuaded that it is only the gospel of peace which can raise the degenerate sons of Adam."

Mary Moffat taught in the primary school at Kuruman and gave birth to ten children, though not all lived beyond infancy. The Moffats also adopted three native children whom they rescued from being buried alive with their dead mothers.

The Moffats returned to England to raise funds and recruit workers for the mission. Dr. David Livingstone answered the call and later, in Africa, met and married the Moffats' daughter, Mary. While in England the elder Mary wrote to her husband to say she longed "to get home to see again where we so long toiled and suffered, to see our beloved companions in the toils and sufferings, and to behold our swarthy brethren and sisters again."

In 1870 the Moffats retired from the mission field. Shortly after their return to England, Mary died; and Robert mourned, "For fifty-three years, I have had her to pray for me!"

Lord, I pray for myself and ask on behalf of all your loving believers—let mutual love continue among us. We are hungry for true fellowship in the faith.

RELATED SCRIPTURE READING— HEBREWS 13:1

PART 4

THE
MARTYRS

ANNE ASKEW

(CA. 1521–1546)

O Lord! I have more enemies now than there be hairs on my head; yet, Lord, let them never overcome me with vain words, but fight thou, Lord, in my stead; for on thee I cast my care. With all the spite they can imagine they fall upon me, who am thy poor creature. Yet, sweet Lord, let me not set by them that are against me; for in thee is my delight. And, Lord, I heartily desire of thee, that thou wilt of thy merciful goodness forgive them that violence which they do, and have done unto me. Open also their blind hearts, that they may hereafter do that thing in thy sight which is only acceptable before thee, and so set forth thy verity aright, without all vain fantasies of sinful men. So be it, Lord.

A PRAYER OF ANNE ASKEW

The English Protestant martyr Anne Askew once said that she would rather read five lines in the Bible than hear five masses in the temple. She denied the Catholic doctrine of transubstantiation, which says that the bread and wine of communion are changed by ritual into the actual body and blood of Christ. Her husband, a Catholic, put her out of his house for her religious beliefs. She traveled to London and joined with other Protestants, was arrested, and brought before the Lord Mayor who asked, "Thou foolish woman, sayest thou, that the priests cannot make the body of Christ?" She answered: "I say so, my Lord; for I have read that God made man; but that man can make God, I never yet read, nor, I suppose, ever shall read." After imprisonment at Newgate and torture in the Tower of London, Askew was burned at the stake.

When the apostle Paul wrote his second letter to Timothy, he was expecting to die soon. He was to be beheaded, presumably for telling people of a God besides the Roman emperor. From prison Paul wrote his final letter saying, "As for me, . . . the time of my departure has come. I have fought the good fight, I have finished the race, I have kept the faith. From now on there is reserved for me the crown of righteousness, which the Lord, the righteous judge, will give me on that day, and not only to me but also *to all who have longed for his appearing*" (2 Timothy 4:6–8, italics added).

Paul set the pattern for martyrdom. At his end he revealed no bitterness toward those who betrayed him. He did not condemn his persecutors. Instead he looked forward to the reward that is to be given to all those who long for the Lord and his return. This longing has to do with loving. It is a loving desire for a real person.

Such love is visible in Anne Askew's prayer. Though she mentions her enemies' vain words and spite, she prays that they be forgiven and enlightened. The heart of her prayer is in these words: "Sweet Lord, let me not set by them that are against me; for in thee is my delight."

The secret of Askew's prayer is love for God in Christ. She did not hope to be delivered from enemies who numbered more than the hairs on her head. By the age of twenty-five she had lost her husband, her home, and her two children and was about to lose her life, not for the sake of a doctrine but for the love of God whom she named sweet Lord.

Here is the secret of endurance in the faith—not correctness or strength or even knowledge—it is love for the one who is coming.

Dear Lord, I am not Anne Askew. I have no enemies like hers. I have not suffered the torturer's rack. But I pray that love like hers will grow in me so that when I face the end of my days I may tell you, "Sweet Lord, in thee is my delight."

RELATED SCRIPTURE READING—REVELATION 22:20

MARY DYER

(D. 1660)

Mary Dyer
Quaker
Witness For Religious Freedom
Hanged on Boston Common 1660

"My life not availeth me
in comparison to the
liberty of the Truth."

INSCRIPTION ON THE MONUMENT TO MARY DYER,
WHICH OVERLOOKS BOSTON COMMON

Mary Dyer came to Boston from England in 1635 with her husband William, a milliner. They were members of Boston's First Church and associated with Anne Hutchinson, who opposed the Calvinist doctrine of predestination and the Puritan hierarchy. When Hutchinson was excommunicated, the Dyers were banished from the colony and settled in Newport, Rhode Island.

In 1652 the couple went with Roger Williams, founder of the colony, to England to procure a charter for Rhode Island. There Mary Dyer converted to Quakerism and stayed on in England for four years.

Meanwhile Quakers had so stirred the wrath of the Puritan theocratic authorities that when Dyer returned to Massachusetts, she was arrested and jailed. After three months she was released and returned to Newport. The next year Dyer and others were arrested while visiting imprisoned Quakers in Boston. Brought to trial, Dyer and two other Quakers were condemned to death by Governor Endicott.

Schoolchildren learn that America was founded on high principles, including free speech, freedom of assembly, and the separation of church and state. Yet these very principles considered foundational to liberty were an offense to the religious ortho-doxy of the Puritans of the seventeenth century.

Why was Mary Dyer martyred? Because these Puritan leaders alone decreed the content of the Christian faith for the citizens of the Massachusetts Bay Colony. They violently opposed any view besides their own. Their most notable victim is Roger Williams, who angered the Anglican Puritans of Massachusetts because he insisted that the king's land patent was invalid. He maintained that only direct purchase from the Indians gave a just title to land. He also held that civil magistrates had no right to interfere in matters of religion. He was banished from the colony and in 1636 founded Rhode Island.

On October 25, 1659, a huge crowd gathered to watch the exe-cution of William Robinson, Marmaduke Stephenson, and Mary Dyer. Dyer, bound and with a noose about her neck, watched as her companions were hanged from a large elm tree on Boston Common. Then, at the last minute, she was reprieved and returned to prison. But Dyer refused to stop preaching. Banished from Mass-achusetts, she was back again six months later. Arrested and brought to court, she was hanged on June 1, 1660.

Mary Dyer is buried in an unmarked grave on Boston Com-mon. One day you may walk across the Common; if you do, remember the woman who paid the highest price for the liber-ties that you unconsciously enjoy every day. And say a prayer for liberty and for those who today, all around the world, strug-gle against oppression, knowing that their lives do not avail in comparison to the freedom of the truth.

Dear God, I am humbled by the story of Mary Dyer! I can only bow in thanks to you for the liberties that make life possible in America. Strengthen this country's resolve to protect, maintain, and spread true freedom throughout the world.

RELATED SCRIPTURE READING—ACTS 5:33–39

ANNE HUTCHINSON

(1591–1643)

> This tablet is placed here in honor of Anne Hutchinson, born in Lincolnshire, England, about 1592; received into membership of this church 1634; banished from Massachusetts by decree of court 1637; killed by the Indians at Pelham, New York, 1643; a breeder of heresies, of ready wit and bold spirit. She was a persuasive advocate of the right of independent judgment.
>
> COMMEMORATIVE TABLET AT FIRST CHURCH OF BOSTON

In 1637 the First Church of Boston excommunicated Anne Hutchinson for heresy. In 1904, 266 years later, a tablet bearing the above inscription was affixed to the church building.

Anne Marbury, the daughter of a controversial clergyman, married William Hutchinson, a dealer in textiles, and they lived in Lincolnshire, England. Anne gave birth to fourteen children. During these years in England, Hutchinson broke with the established church, went about listening to many preachers, and studied the newly published King James Version of the Bible.

John Cotton, who greatly influenced Hutchinson's spiritual development, fled England for Boston in 1633. To remain in contact with Cotton, the Hutchinsons emigrated to America the next year, settling in Boston. There, Hutchinson formed midweek classes to discuss Cotton's teachings and to teach the Scriptures, especially to women. Hutchinson's friendship with Cotton and her service as a nurse gained status for her in the community.

She taught a mystical interpretation of Puritan theology. This was supported by some ministers while others feared her opinions would undermine the theocratic structures of Puritan society.

In 1637, when Hutchinson was forty-six, she was charged with heresy and sedition and brought before a synod. Her pastor, John Wilson, pronounced the sentence: "I command you in the name of Christ Jesus and of this church as a leper to withdraw yourself out of this congregation." As she left the church building, Hutchinson said, "The Lord does not judge as man judges. Better to be cast out of the church than to deny Christ."

Anne Hutchinson was excommunicated after a series of ecclesiastical trials. She deftly employed biblical argument and penetrating logic to defend herself against the colony's most powerful ministers and magistrates. "Why should I be condemned?" she asked them. "I conceive there is a clear rule in Titus that elder women should instruct the younger" (Titus 2:3–5). Skillful answers such as these silenced her opponents. But her claim that the Holy Spirit communicated to her directly was intolerable. From a thorough knowledge of the Bible, Hutchinson argued that a believer who possesses the Holy Spirit was not obligated by laws of conduct but was controlled by inner spiritual compulsions. "The Spirit within," she said, "controls the right actions of man. He who has God's grace in his heart cannot go astray."

But her accusers claimed she taught antinomianism, holding that faith is the only necessity for salvation. The very thought of this was anathema to the fundamentalists of early New England. In many ways they resembled the ancient Pharisees—Jesus' persecutors—more than the disciples of Christ. Their criticism of Hutchinson may not have been entirely about her teachings. Its source lay, at least in part, in jealousy over her success and popularity. Sixty to eighty people attended the lectures at her home inconveniently located opposite the colonial governor's house.

Anne Hutchinson was among the first Americans to fight for religious liberty. The principles of free speech, civil liberty, and religious freedom, for which Anne Hutchinson was an early sufferer, are now written into the Constitution of the United States.

Dear God, in these days when the freedoms I enjoy are being challenged and reformed, I pray for my country. Cause her political and business leaders to be restrained by history so that the precious freedoms won by my forebears will not be lost to future generations.

RELATED SCRIPTURE READING—ACTS 17:1–6

NARCISSA WHITMAN

(1808–1847)

September 3, 1836—Here we are all at Walla Walla, through
the mercy of a kind Providence, in health and all our lives preserved. What cause for gratitude and praise to God! Surely my
heart is ready to leap for joy at the thought of being so near the
long-desired work of teaching the benighted ones the knowledge of a Savior, and having completed this hazardous journey
under such favorable circumstances. . . . Another cause for gratitude is the preservation of our animals, in this difficult, dangerous and lengthy route, while many parties previous to ours
have had every animal taken from them, and been left on foot
in a dangerous land, exposed to death.

FROM THE DIARY OF NARCISSA WHITMAN

Born in Plattsburg, New York, Narcissa Prentiss attended the
Female Seminary of Emma Willard in Troy, New York, and the
Benjamin Franklin Academy at Plattsburg. She married Marcus Whitman, a Presbyterian missionary physician, in 1836 and
they immediately left for Old Oregon.

In February 1836, traveling with missionary couple Henry
and Eliza Spaulding, the Whitmans left Ithaca, New York, and
went overland to the Ohio River. By boat they traveled down
the Ohio and up the Mississippi and Missouri Rivers, arriving
near present-day Omaha, Nebraska, in mid-May. There they
joined an American Fur Company caravan for the remaining
nineteen hundred miles to the confluence of the Walla Walla
and Columbia Rivers. Narcissa and Eliza were the lone women
in a party made up of seventy men, and four hundred animals.
The group moved about twenty miles a day. Today in a remote
section of Wyoming stands a stone monument commemorating
Narcissa Whitman and Eliza Spaulding as the first white women
to travel across the Rocky Mountains.

The Whitmans made their home at Waiilatpu in the Walla Walla valley; there they began their mission work. Their nearest non-native neighbors were the Spauldings, 125 miles northeast. In 1837 Narcissa Whitman gave birth to a daughter, Clarissa. The child drowned two years later.

This woman's life was like that of all pioneer women. There was much hardship and hard labor. In addition, Whitman labored in spreading the gospel among the neighboring Cayuse people. Plus, she took in and raised orphaned native and pioneer children.

In 1842 Marcus Whitman returned to New York on mission business, returning in 1843 with a group of one thousand immigrants—the largest influx of pioneers up to that time. By then the Oregon Trail was fully open for western migration. In 1846 Narcissa Whitman oversaw the care of sixty-nine people at the mission.

In 1847 an epidemic of measles caused so many fatalities among the Cayuse that they suspected the Whitmans and other missionaries of using evil power against them. On November 29, 1847, a handful of Indians entered the Whitman home and killed Marcus and Narcissa. Twelve others were killed in the attack, including some of the Whitmans' adopted children.

Narcissa Whitman's last words were, "Tell my sister that I died at my post." Like countless others, she imitated the apostle Paul, the church's first missionary, who was poured out like a drink offering in the service of the gospel (see 2 Timothy 4:6). As he said, "I have fought the good fight, I have finished the race, I have kept the faith" (v. 7).

O Lord, I am surrounded by an immense, invisible crowd of people who have been faithful to testify for you! Many of them have died doing so—like Narcissa Whitman. I pray for perseverance to run faith's race as I look to you, the pioneer and perfecter of my faith.

RELATED SCRIPTURE READING—REVELATION 1:9

PART 5

THE POETS

ANNE BRADSTREET

(1612–1672)

May 13, 1657

My winter's past, my storms are gone,
And former clouds seem now all fled,
But if they must eclipse again,
I'll run where I was succored.

I have a shelter from the storm,
A shadow from the fainting heat,
I have access unto his throne,
Who is a God so wondrous great.

O hath thou made my pilgrimage
Thus pleasant, fair, and good,
Blessed me in youth and elder age,
My Baca made a springing flood.

O studious am what I shall do
To show my duty with delight;
All I can give is but thine own
And at the most a simple mite.

FROM A POEM BY ANNE BRADSTREET

Raised in cultured circumstances, Anne Dudley married Simon Bradstreet, a protégé of the Earl of Lincoln, while still in her teen years. Two years later the couple migrated to the Massachusetts Bay Colony. Thomas Dudley, Anne's father, was the second governor of the colony, and her husband would become governor seven years after her death. Anne Bradstreet raised eight children, was hostess for her husband, and wrote poetry, becoming the first published poet of the American colonies.

Her brother-in-law arranged for the publication of Anne's poems in England under the title *The Tenth Muse Lately Sprung Up in America* (1650). Finding critical acceptance in the twenty-first century, her poetry is still read today.

The final stanza of Bradstreet's poem given here states a familiar dilemma: God has given me so much, and I have so little to give him in return. The poet knows that all she has is God's in the first place and concludes that she will give a symbolic gift represented by the widow's mite (see Mark 12:41–44).

Another poet, Christina Rossetti, asks in her well-known Christmas poem "In the Bleak Midwinter," "What can I give him / Poor as I am?" Rossetti decides to give God her heart.

An ancient Hebrew poet also wondered, "What shall I return to the LORD for all his bounty to me?" (Psalm 116:12). One may expect that a Jew would automatically know the answer and immediately tithe a percentage of all his earnings. Many modern Christians do the same.

Here we have three possible answers of what to give to God: 1. Bradstreet's symbolic gift, since God has no need. 2. Rossetti's devotional gift of love—her heart. 3. A fixed monetary gift in the offering plate. All three are valid and wonderful. But the poet of Psalm 116 answered the question in quite a surprising way. "I will lift up the cup of salvation," he sang, "and call on the name of the LORD" (v. 13).

We Christians lift such a cup regularly; as Paul wrote, "He took the cup also, after supper, saying, 'This cup is the new covenant in my blood. Do this, as often as you drink it, in remembrance of me.' For as often as you eat this bread and drink the cup, you proclaim the Lord's death until he comes" (1 Corinthians 11:25–26). A believer in Christ gives God the gift of remembrance until he comes again and, drinking the cup of the Lord's Table, gives thanks.

Lord, thank you for all you have given me. Make it possible that throughout my life I can take the cup of salvation and with joy call on your name.

RELATED SCRIPTURE READING—LUKE 22:14–20

ANNE BRADSTREET

ADVICE TO HER SON

It is admirable to consider the power of faith, by which all things are (almost) possible to be done; it can remove mountains (if need were); it hath stayed the course of the sun, raised the dead, cast out devils, reversed the order of nature, quenched the violence of the fire, made the water become firm footing for Peter to walk on; nay, more than all these it hath overcome the omnipotent Himself, as when Moses intercedes for the people, God saith to him, "Let me alone, that I may destroy them," as if Moses had been able by the hand of faith to hold the everlasting arms of the mighty God of Jacob. Yea Jacob himself when he wrestled with God face to face in Penuel, "Let me go," saith that Angel. "I will not let thee go," replies Jacob, "till thou bless me." Faith is not only thus potent but it is so necessary that without faith there is no salvation; therefore with all our seekings and gettings, let us above all seek to obtain this pearl of price.

FROM A LETTER BY ANNE BRADSTREET TO HER SON

Anne and Simon Bradstreet were among twelve English families who banded together to help found the Massachusetts Bay Colony. Led by John Winthrop, they sailed for the New World from Southampton in 1630. Anne Bradstreet was eighteen years old.

After a seventy-two-day voyage, rife with sickness, she viewed the springtime shore of Massachusetts. The group settled in Cambridge and may have lived the summer in wigwams and hillside dugouts. The Bradstreets built their house on the present-day site of Harvard Square. In time the family moved to Andover where they raised eight children and Anne wrote remarkable poetry. All but one of the Bradstreet children were living when Anne, age 60, died of tuberculosis.

This woman sailed away from the comfort of the estates of the Earl of Lincoln to pioneer the wilderness of New England.

Her life would have been significant even if she had not become America's first published poet. But without her poetry Anne Bradstreet's name would be but a single note in the symphony of early American history.

Bradstreet once wrote to her oldest child, Simon: "You once desired me to leave something for you in writing that you might look upon, when you should see me no more; I could think of nothing more fit for you nor of more ease to myself than these short meditations following"—her seventy-seven "Meditations Divine and Moral"—short aphorisms and observations on life ranging in length from a single sentence ("Authority without wisdom is like a heavy axe without an edge: fitter to bruise than polish") to long paragraphs.

Bradstreet told her son, "Such as they are, I bequeath to you; small legacies are accepted by true friends, much more by dutiful children." Bradstreet's legacy gives pause for a person to consider what he or she is leaving for loved ones to "look upon, when you should see me no more."

In one of my photo albums there is a photo of my maternal great-grandmother, Eliza, who flourished to age 104. It is a wonderful photo—an old woman in a rocker on a porch. But it is all we have of her. There is another photo somewhere of Eliza's father taken in a studio when he served in the Civil War. But there are also letters that he wrote home from the war. To me, the letters are more precious than the photo; they tell so much more of him.

Anne Bradstreet's grave site is unknown. No portrait of her exists. Yet she is known through her writings. It is a way we all can be known as we write letters to those we love—letters of significance telling of ourselves, our beliefs, our feelings, and observations about life and the world. A small legacy indeed, yet accepted with love by true friends and dutiful children.

Lord, thank you for the people who love me. Help me to open my heart to them in love and truth that this might be my heritage to them.

RELATED SCRIPTURE READING—1 JOHN 2:12–13

ELIZABETH BARRETT BROWNING

(1806–1861)

I think that look of Christ might seem to say,
"Thou Peter! Art thou then a common stone
Which I at last must break my heart upon,
For all God's charge to his high angels may
Guard my foot better? Did I yesterday
Wash thy feet, my beloved, that they should run
Quick to deny me 'neath the morning sun?
And do thy kisses, like the rest, betray?
The cock crows coldly.—Go, and manifest
A late contrition, but no bootless fear!
For when thy final need is dreariest,
Thou shalt not be denied, as I am here;
My voice to God and angels shall attest,
'Because I *know* this man, let him be clear.'"

A POEM BY ELIZABETH BARRETT BROWNING

This poem expresses one of the most common themes of literature and the Bible—redemption. The power of the Christian
faith is the force of Christ's genuine redemption. This indem-
nity from death no one can purchase, earn, or construct. Look
at Peter, our model, our example. As the poet tells it, Christ says
to him, "Did I yesterday / Wash thy feet, my beloved, that they
should run / Quick to deny me 'neath the morning sun?" One
evening Jesus is humbly washing Peter's feet (John 13:6–9). The
next morning Peter is denying that he knows the man (Matthew
26:69–75). If you think, *I would not do that*, you are self-deceived.

When the rooster crowed, Peter realized what he had done.
He was suddenly hopeless. "And he went out and wept bitterly"
(v. 75). Much occurs before the final line of the poem—Christ
dies and accomplishes redemption. He dries every bitter tear.

With the price of his life, Christ purchased all of humanity and the entire creation for God.

What will Christ say to God about you "when thy final need is dreariest"? As Elizabeth Barrett Browning tells it, "Thou shalt not be denied. . . ." Christ will say this: "I *know* this man, let him be clear."

Though her life is immortalized in the play *The Barretts of Wimpole Street*, Elizabeth Barrett Browning is often remembered simply as the wife of Robert Browning, who also happened to write sonnets about their love. But she was an accomplished and popular poet in her own right; more popular in fact than her husband. Her later poems on social injustice, slave trade in America, the oppression of the Italians by the Austrians, child labor, and oppression of women are hardly the yield of a weak romantic. In addition to her skill as a poet, she was a lifelong student, translator, abolitionist, and early feminist. She was also active in Italian politics. Although her popularity waned after her death, today Barrett Browning's poetry, especially "Aurora Leigh" (1856), is valued and studied as classic literature. Here are a few lines from this lengthy poem:

> Earth's crammed with heaven,
> And every common bush afire with God;
> But only he who sees, takes off his shoes,
> The rest sit round it and pluck blackberries,
> And daub their natural faces unaware
> More and more from the first similitude.

Dearest Lord Jesus, with all of my heart, as little as it is, I thank you for redemption. By the powerful fact of your death I give myself again to be alive to God to whom you safely delivered me.

RELATED SCRIPTURE READING—GALATIANS 2:20

FRANCES HAVERGAL

(1836–1879)

Dear blind sister over the sea,
An English heart goes forth to thee.
We are linked by a cable of faith and song
Flashing bright sympathy swift along:
One in the East and one in the West
Singing for him whom our souls love best;
"Singing for Jesus," telling his love
All the way to our home above,
Where the severing sea with its restless tide,
Never shall hinder and never divide.
Sister! What shall our meeting be,
When our hearts shall sing, and our eyes shall see!

FRANCES HAVERGAL'S POEM TO FANNY CROSBY

Frances Ridley Havergal is called the "consecration poet" because her hymns often emphasize complete dedication to God. Significantly her namesake is Nicholas Ridley, a prominent bishop martyred at Oxford in 1555.

She was born in Astely, Worcestershire, England, where her father, William H. Havergal, was rector. He was also a composer of cathedral music, chants, tunes, and sacred songs. In frail health, Frances Havergal was educated at home and in private schools in England and Germany. She was a natural linguist, mastering French, German, Italian, Latin, Greek, and Hebrew. This extraordinary woman was a devoted Bible student who memorized large portions of Scripture. She also practiced a disciplined prayer life and noted in her Bible the times and topics of her prayers.

Havergal inherited her father's musical gift. She was a pianist and especially enjoyed interpreting Handel, Mendelssohn, and Beethoven. Her singing voice matched the beauty of the hymns she wrote, which number about fifty. These include "Thou Art

Coming, O My Savior," "Take My Life and Let It Be," "Who Is on the Lord's Side?" and "Like a River Glorious." She also authored some two hundred poems, posthumously published in *Poetical Works* (1884).

Frances Havergal described her way of writing hymns like this: "Writing is praying with me, for I never seem to write even a verse by myself. . . . I ask that at every line He would give me not merely thoughts and power, but also every word, even the very rhymes."

The hymnist surely found agreement in her "dear blind sister over the sea," Fanny Crosby, who, like Havergal, had no doubt that some of her hymns were dictated by the Holy Spirit.

Havergal's poetic note to Crosby calls out, "Sister! What shall our meeting be, / When our hearts shall sing, and our eyes shall see!" —a loving reference to Crosby's temporal blindness and a hopeful reminder of their shared life in eternity when "we will see face to face" (1 Corinthians 13:12).

What sights will we see in eternity? This is not truly known. Even the apostle Paul could claim only to see dimly, as if he was peering through his own reflection in a darkened window.

However, in the Book of Revelation, John states directly, "Then I saw a new heaven and a new earth" (21:1). Still, he describes eternity only in allegory: "And I saw the holy city, the new Jerusalem, coming down out of heaven from God, prepared as a bride adorned for her husband" (v. 2). Similarly, the next chapter begins, "The angel showed me the river of the water of life, bright as crystal, flowing from the throne of God and of the Lamb" (22:1). What is this? An actual river or a picture to describe something spiritual? It is hard to say.

What can be said is what already has been said, "What no eye has seen, nor ear heard, nor the human heart conceived, what God has prepared for those who love him" (1 Corinthians 2:9).

Lord, I can see only through a glass darkly but I long to see face-to-face. Now I know only in part. Oh! how I want to know fully, even as I have been fully known.

RELATED SCRIPTURE READING—1 JOHN 3:2

CHRISTINA ROSSETTI

(1830–1894)

Thou are Thyself my goal, O Lord my King:
Stretch forth Thy hand to save my soul:
What matters more or less of journeying?
While I touch Thee I touch my goal,
O Sweet Jesu.

"SLAIN FROM THE FOUNDATION OF THE WORLD"
(LINES 18–22)

Christina Rossetti began to write poetry at an early age, and in 1847 her grandfather printed a volume of her verse. Born in London, Rossetti was a member of the Anglican church and was often busy with church work and the preparation of devotional manuals.

"Uphill" was the first of Rossetti's poems to receive wide attention. It tells of a steep climb with a comfortable inn at the top—a parable of salvation. "A Royal Princess" deals with starvation, inequality, and poverty, and appeared in an 1863 anthology published for the relief of victims of the Lancashire cotton famine. Rossetti was considered as a possible successor to Alfred, Lord Tennyson, the poet laureate. The honor went to William Wordsworth instead.

In 1871 Rossetti was diagnosed with the thyroid disorder called Graves' disease, which marred her appearance and endangered her life. In addition to physical troubles, she was emotionally weakened when her brother, the painter Dante Gabriel Rossetti had a mental breakdown in 1872. Christina Rossetti developed cancer in 1891 and died at her London residence.

In her poem "Slain from the Foundation of the World" Ms. Rossetti expresses a very simple idea, yet one that is of utmost importance to a person's growth in the faith. As the psalmist wrote,

"Whom have I in heaven but you? And there is nothing on earth that I desire other than you" (73:25). The psalmist seems to see only the Lord.

This is just as Jesus Christ said, "Your eye is the lamp of your body. If your eye is healthy, your whole body is full of light" (Luke 11:34). A person with a healthy eye can see where she is going and is not easily distracted from her goal, even though there are many excellent distractions! For example, blessings. There are spiritual blessings—gifts of healing, insight; physical blessings—health, stature; and personal blessings—family, employment. And how about the distraction of feelings?—happiness, peace, joy. Or activities—prayer, Bible study, giving.

Every one of these things is good. Yet not one of them is Christ. These blessings certainly have their source in God, but if a believer seeks such blessings, he or she has been diverted from the goal of the faith. Christ is himself the blessing.

For a person going home at Thanksgiving, is the goal a turkey dinner? No. The Thanksgiving meal is found at home; but even if there were no meal, home is the goal. As Rossetti wrote, "While I touch Thee I touch my goal, / O Sweet Jesu."

Consider Paul. If anyone was blessed, it was he: "Circumcised on the eighth day, a member of the people of Israel, of the tribe of Benjamin, a Hebrew born of Hebrews; as to the law, a Pharisee; as to zeal, a persecutor of the church; as to righteousness under the law, blameless" (Philippians 3:5–6). Paul let this all go for one reason—"Whatever gains I had, these I have come to regard as loss . . . because of the surpassing value of knowing Christ Jesus my Lord. . . . this one thing I do: forgetting what lies behind and straining forward to what lies ahead, I press on toward the goal for the prize of the heavenly call of God in Christ Jesus" (vv. 7, 8, 13, 14).

Heavenly Father, save me from the thought that I have already obtained the knowledge of Christ, that I have already reached the goal. Energize me to press on to make him my own because Christ has made me his own.

RELATED SCRIPTURE READING—HEBREWS 12:1–2

FANNY CROSBY

(1820–1915)

That some of my hymns have been dictated by the blessed Holy Spirit, I have no doubt. That others have been the result of deep meditation, I know to be true. But that the poet has any right to claim special merit for himself is certainly presumptuous. I have sometimes felt that there is a deep and clear well of inspiration from which one may draw the sparkling draughts that are so essential to good poetry. At times the burden of inspiration is so heavy that the author himself cannot find words beautiful enough or thoughts deep enough for its expression.

FANNY CROSBY

Frances (Fanny) Jane Crosby is the most beloved and celebrated of American hymn writers. She was born in Putnam County, New York, and became blind at the age of six weeks due to a physician's malpractice.

In 1835 she entered the New York City Institution for the Blind and completed twelve years of training there. Crosby then served on the faculty of the institution from 1847 to 1858. She was twenty-four years old when her first book was published: *The Blind Girl and Other Poems*. She had also written lyrics to several popular songs.

Crosby became a Christian when she was thirty-one years old. In 1858 she married the musician Alexander Van Alstyne, also blind, whose assistance contributed greatly to his wife's success.

But Crosby was forty-four before she wrote her first hymn. At that time she met the well-known composer William Bradbury, who suggested that she attempt to write a hymn for him. She soon delivered to Bradbury her first sacred song, which begins:

We are going, we are going to a home beyond the skies,
Where the fields are robed in beauty,
And the sunlight never dies.

84

Under her own name, as well as using some two hundred pen names, Fanny Crosby wrote the lyrics to more than two thousand hymns. Her lyrics are simple and easy to remember, and her songs are not strongly associated with a particular denomination or movement. They are, it seems, everyone's hymns.

Ira Sankey, song leader for D. L. Moody, popularized Crosby's hymns during the Moody-Sankey revivals of the late nineteenth century. The crowds who thronged these meetings sang her songs, and they became the heritage of a generation. There is hardly a hymnbook in the English language that does not contain at least one hymn by Fanny Crosby.

It is difficult to overstate the value of such hymns to the Christian faith. Our tradition of hymns originates in the New Testament itself—the Lord's Last Supper ended with the singing of a hymn (Matthew 26:30); the apostles sang hymns on their journeys (Acts 16:25); the churches sang hymns in their meetings (1 Corinthians 14:26); believers sang individually (James 5:13); the apostle Paul quoted hymns in his epistles (Philippians 2:6–11) and urged believers to sing: "Be filled with the Spirit . . . singing and making melody to the Lord in your hearts" (Ephesians 5:18–19).

These words of the apostle provide much information about singing: It issues from a heart filled with the Spirit and is a way for one's heart to be filled. All kinds of songs will do—long or short, profound or simple, hymn or chorus. This is not performance for others; though we may sing together, among ourselves, we do not sing to each other; we sing to the Lord. And certainly Fanny Crosby would expect that we follow the charge of this verse and sing with our heart—with sincere love for God.

Thank you, Father, for the rich heritage of music that I enjoy in your church. May every hymn be sung to you with hearts filled with your Spirit.

RELATED SCRIPTURE READING—PSALM 40:1–3

PART 6

THE
PROPHETS

HILDEGARD OF BINGEN

(1098–1179)

I, flaming Life of the divine substance, flare up above the
beauty of the plains, I shine in the waters and blaze in the sun,
the moon and the stars, and with an airy wind, as if by an invisible life which sustains the whole, I arouse all things to life. . . .
I am Life whole and entire; . . . all that is living is rooted in me.
For Reason is the root and in it blossoms the resounding Word.

A PROPHECY OF HILDEGARD OF BINGEN

The life of Hildegard of Bingen spanned most of the twelfth century. It is an important study in medieval history and culture and
is an inspirational chronicle of a spirit and intellect that over-
came social, physical, cultural, and gender barriers, which are
inconceivable to the modern mind.

Hildegard was born to noble parents in Mainz in what is now
Germany. At a young age she was sent to be educated at a Benedictine monastery. There Hildegard was tutored by the sole female
resident, Jutta. She studied Latin, the Bible, and perhaps music.

In 1136 Jutta died, and the women who had gathered there
elected Hildegard to lead them. This community of the daughters and widows of well-to-do families flourished and Hildegard
rose to prominence. When Hildegard was forty-two years old,
intense visions of God caused her to become bedridden. Persuaded to publish her revelations, she wrote *Scivias (Know the
Ways)*, a classic of medieval mysticism.

Hildegard was well-known in Germany and beyond. Her
ecclesiastical music was used in other regions, she traveled widely
as a teacher and preacher, and she wrote books on science, medicine, hymnody, theology, and biography.

Hildegard saw music as the means of recapturing the joy and
beauty of paradise. Her view was that before the fall, Adam had

a pure voice and joined angels in singing God's praise. Music was invented and musical instruments were made only after the fall, for use in worship of God.

In the days of Hildegard the Bible was not available, and most people were illiterate. This is why pictures and statues and songs came to be used in the church to tell the gospel. In mid–seventh century England, for example, an Anglo-Saxon monk named Caedmon, influenced by a dream, began to sing the stories of creation, of Israel, and more. He went about singing, and his songs became a sort of people's Bible. They had no other.

Perhaps Hildegard's visions were similar, a way for God to be known in the preliterate days of our history. Read the above words of Hildegard and compare them with those of John:

> In the beginning was the Word, and the Word was with God, and the Word was God. He was in the beginning with God. All things came into being through him, and without him not one thing came into being. What has come into being in him was life, and the life was the light of all people. The light shines in the darkness, and the darkness did not overcome it.
>
> JOHN 1:1–5

Hildegard's era is sometimes called the Dark Ages. But she was a courageous woman of the light, willing to speak and sing for God in a time plagued by little knowledge of the gospel. Her active mind, diligence, and love of God made her a leader in the Middle Ages; still today Hildegard of Bingen bears a timeless transcendence.

O Light of the world, thank you that I possess the knowledge of the truth about who you are and what you have done for my world. Give me courage like Hildegard's so that I may make this good news known to those around me.

RELATED SCRIPTURE READING—ACTS 16:13–15

CATHERINE OF SIENA

(1347–1380)

Merciful Lord, it does not surprise me that you forget completely the sins of those who repent. I am not surprised that you remain faithful to those who hate and revile you. The mercy which pours forth from you fills the whole world.

It was by your mercy that we were created, and by your mercy that you redeemed us by sending your Son. . . . Your justice is constantly tempered with mercy. So you refuse to punish us as we deserve. O mad lover! It was not enough for you to take on your humanity; you had to die for us as well.

A PRAYER OF CATHERINE OF SIENA

Catherine du Giacomo di Benincasa was one of the younger of twenty-five children born to a wealthy dyer of Siena. At the age of sixteen she became a Dominican lay sister, leading a strict ascetic life in her own home. Later she became a nurse and led an active public life of menial service, ecclesiastical reform, and political diplomacy. A highly intelligent, spiritual, and devout medieval nun, Catherine had a reputation for insight and sound judgment and, although almost illiterate, dictated letters that influenced many.

Catherine of Siena's book *The Dialogue* is her spiritual testament. It begins: "A soul rises up, restless with tremendous desire for God's honor and the salvation of souls. . . . she seeks to pursue truth and clothes herself in it." The book, a dialogue between a soul and God, overflows with allegory. Its layers of symbols and variety of metaphors attempt to describe the indescribable.

This woman was surely enthralled with God's love for her. This accounts for her freedom to call God "O mad lover!" Look at this madness: "It was not enough for you to take on your humanity," says Catherine; "you had to die for us as well."

Christianity, of course, is not the only religion to believe in a suffering God-man. For example, the Egyptians worshiped Osiris who, they believed, died and rose again. The problem is that these events took place in some mythical era of prehistory. In contrast, the life and death of Jesus Christ occurred *within* history. Scholars know when Jesus was born—at the same time Caesar Augustus decided to levy a tax on his empire (Luke 2:1). This date is as concrete as is the year of the signing of the Declaration of Independence (1776).

Christ died at the hands of Pontius Pilate, who was governor of Judea between A.D. 26 and 36. So when the Bible says that "they asked Pilate to have him killed" (Acts 13:28), it is something like the *New York Times* reporting that President Ford pardoned Richard Nixon.

There may have been Egyptians four or five millennia past who called Osiris their lover. But we know that this is not at all uncommon among modern Christians. Such love for God fulfills the requirements of the law (Matthew 22:36–40).

Jesus Christ is so intimate and real, he inspires a heart to sing:

> Hast thou heard him, seen him, known him?
> Is not thine a captured heart?
> Chief among ten thousand own him;
> Joyful choose the better part.
>> Captivated by his beauty,
>> All my heart's love haste to bring;
>> Let his peerless worth constrain thee,
>> Crown him now unrivaled king.

ANONYMOUS

Dearest Lord Jesus Christ, I pray that the love in my heart for you may increase. But not only in my heart, in the hearts of all your believers as well, so that this love can be told wherever the good news is proclaimed.

RELATED SCRIPTURE READING—MATTHEW 26:6–13

JULIAN OF NORWICH

(CA. 1342–CA. 1413)

One time our Lord said to me, "All things shall be well." And another time he said, "You yourself shall see that all manner of things shall be well," and my soul understood these two sayings to mean several different things.

One meaning was that his will is for us to know that he takes notice not only of great and noble things, but of little and small things as well, low and simple things, one and the other. . . .

Another meaning was this: We see many evil deeds done all around us, deeds that cause great harm, and sometimes it seems impossible that they should ever result in anything good. Sometimes when we see these evils, sorrowing and mourning because of them, we find it difficult to concentrate on beholding God blissfully, . . . the cause of this is that our reasoning capacity is not so blind, low, and simple that we cannot know his high and marvelous wisdom, the power and the goodness of the blissful Trinity. And this is what he meant when he said, "You yourself shall see that all manner of things shall be well." It was as if he had said, "Take heed faithfully and trustingly now, and at the end of all things, you will truly see them in the fullness of joy."

A REVELATION OF JULIAN OF NORWICH

Julian of Norwich lived a solitary life of prayer and meditation near Saint Julian's Church, Norwich, England. Little is known about her besides what she wrote in *Revelations of Divine Love*.

In 1373 Julian was sick and near death for six days. On the seventh she received fifteen revelations. On the eighth day a final vision revealed her soul as a city, an endless world, and also a blessed kingdom with Christ sitting in it. Julian meditated on these visions for twenty years, concentrating on God's love—the answer to all life's problems and to the world's evil. Eventually she wrote the first English literary work published by a woman:

Revelations of Divine Love (1393)—a record of her visions and her meditations on them.

We may suppose that it was simple for Julian to say, "You yourself shall see that all manner of things shall be well." After all, how difficult could things have been for her?

Julian was born into the era of the Black Death—a pandemic of plague, which ravaged Europe between 1347 and 1400 and caused the death of about one-third of Europe's population (roughly twenty-five million people).

Also, the times of Julian of Norwich were devastated by the Hundred Years' War—a recurrent struggle between England and France over various disputes, including the question of the legitimate succession to the French crown. The war's turning point came in 1429 when the English army was compelled by a relief force organized by Joan of Arc to lift its siege of Orléans.

The concerns of contemporary authors pale before those of the obscure anchorite of Norwich. We moderns have a surfeit of self-help books to (supposedly) tell us how to cope. Julian, an unlikely author in any age, gave her world a lucid work of Christian mysticism. In it she follows the lead of the apostle Paul, turning our attention to the Bible's unique point of convergence: "To me, living is Christ" (Philippians 1:21).

Julian wrote:

> Kept secure by Christ we are assured, by his touch of grace, of salvation; broken by Adam's fall, and in many ways by our own sins and sorrows, we are so darkened and blinded that we can hardly find any comfort. But in our heart we abide in God, and confidently trust to his mercy and grace—and this is his working in us.
>
> FROM *REVELATIONS OF DIVINE LOVE*

Thank you, Father, for your Son, Jesus Christ, who loved me and gave himself for me. And thank you so much for all Christ is and can be to me as I live my life.

RELATED SCRIPTURE READING—ROMANS 8:28

JULIAN OF NORWICH

DIVINE LOVE

And from the time that I saw [the vision], I often desired to know what our Lord meant by it. More than fifteen years afterward I was given the answer. . . . It is as follows:

"Would you know your Lord's meaning in this thing? Know it well, love was his meaning. Who showed it to you? Love. What did he show you? Love. Why did he show it? For love. Keep yourself in love and you shall know and understand more in the same. But you shall never know nor understand any other thing, forever." Thus I was taught that love was our Lord's meaning. And I saw quite clearly in this and in all things, that before God made us, he loved us. This love was never diminished nor ever shall it ever be. And in this love he has done all his work.

A REVELATION OF JULIAN OF NORWICH

Julian was not a nun; she was an anchorite—a person called to a solitary life, though not entirely cut off from the world, rather anchored in it while living in prayer and contemplation. Her home was a small room in or near the Church of St. Julian in Norwich, England.

In her time, the Roman Catholic Church was in the midst of the Great Western Schism (1378–1417) when dissidents elected a pope who was seated in Avignon, while a second pope ruled Rome. Religious orders were feuding. It was also at this time that followers of the early Protestant John Wycliffe were tortured and burned in the Lollards' Pit, across the river from St. Julian's Church.

With the plague and wars upending society and the church in turmoil, people throughout Europe had a renewed fear of death and of God. People turned within themselves for religious meaning and many Christian mystics like the gentle Julian of Norwich came on the scene.

In abnormal times God raises up prophets to testify of his divine nature and purpose. History is replete with men and women who maintained and advanced God's testimony. One of the best-known is the courageous Martin Luther, who began the Reformation in the sixteenth century. Its tremors shake society still today.

The church would not exist without its long list of prophets—reformers and revolutionaries, preachers, and people of prayer. Such prophets, greater and lesser, known and unknown, have in their time trimmed the wick in the lantern of the light of the gospel.

Many of the women highlighted in this book are such prophets: Catherine Booth labored for the poor and outcasts of society; Harriet Beecher Stowe distilled America's anguish over institutionalized slavery; and Mary Dyer gave her life to advance religious freedom. Julian of Norwich found opportunity to speak for God by telling her *Revelations of Divine Love*.

Technologically, hers was an entirely different world than ours. But was it similar in some ways? The twentieth century saw death on a massive scale in the European Holocaust, Soviet Stalinist policies, and Mao's revolution. New epidemic diseases replaced plague, and wars seemed ceaseless.

In view of this, one's impulse is to pray. And pray we must. There is no way to know who the next prophet will be, though there is little doubt that it will be a person of prayer. So if you are praying, prepare to be raised up as a prophet. Who knows what your field of labor will be? Luther affected the whole world. Julian may have been heard only in her own neighborhood.

And one day, through prayer and God's purpose, the final prophet will come—the Lord of glory is his name.

My God, thank you for sending the prophets through the ages and for the light of the gospel, which they have kept burning. Speed the day of your return, for which they all waited, when the trumpet will sound and the dead will be raised imperishable and we will be changed.

RELATED SCRIPTURE READING—HEBREWS 12:1–2

CATHERINE OF GENOA

(1447–1510)

At times I have thought that my love was complete, but later, as my sight grew clearer, I became aware that I had many imperfections. I did not recognize them at first because God's love for me has it planned that I will achieve it little by little for the sake of preserving me and keeping me humble so as to be tolerable to myself and others!

Every day I feel the motes in my eyes being removed as God's pure love casts them out. We cannot see these imperfections because if we saw them, we could not bear the sight. Thus, God lets us imagine that we are complete. But never does God cease to remove them. From time to time I feel that I am growing only to see that I still have a long way to go. They become visible to me in the mirror of God's truth of his pure love where everything I thought was straight appears crooked.

FROM *LIFE AND TEACHINGS* BY CATHERINE OF GENOA

Born of nobility, Caterinetta Fieschi entered an arranged marriage in 1463. She was converted to Christianity in 1473, about the time her husband suffered financial setbacks. These brought about his conversion and association with the Third Order of the Franciscans.

Catherine then worked with the Ladies of Mercy in St. Lazarus hospital in Genoa and was the hospital's director from 1490 to 1496. Fasting often, she was known to withdraw from human contact into mystical devotion to God. But she was practical as well as visionary. When plague broke out in Genoa in 1493, she led the city's battle against death by organizing open-air wards of sailcloth tents to receive the sick.

When you read Catherine of Genoa and other medieval Christians, keep in mind that they are pre-Reformation. These people did not pass through the revolutionary changes that came to the faith in the sixteenth and seventeenth centuries. They did not have the benefit of historical hindsight, which we in this century enjoy.

How many books have been written about spiritual growth since Catherine of Genoa wrote her observations in *Life and Teachings?* How many sermons? An untold number. Still, she has genuine understanding to offer on the subject of growth.

Catherine realized that God, in love, planned that believers grow in the faith little by little. No one is born full grown or fully educated. She says that this is "for the sake of preserving me and keeping me humble." Imagine how discouraged you would be if you saw all of your imperfections at once. So gradual growth preserves you. And humility comes from passing through the difficulty and pain that accompany growth in grace. You learn that you are no greater than anyone else and may be somewhat less.

So what is the good of all this preservation and humility? Catherine says, "So as to be tolerable to myself and others!" If you were to see all your imperfections at once, you could not bear the sight—you would be intolerable to yourself. And without humility, you are intolerable to others.

Here is the apostle Peter's description of such growth:

> You must make every effort to support your faith with goodness, and goodness with knowledge, and knowledge with self-control, and self-control with endurance, and endurance with godliness, and godliness with mutual affection, and mutual affection with love. For if these things are yours and are increasing among you, they keep you from being ineffective and unfruitful in the knowledge of our Lord Jesus Christ.
>
> 2 PETER 1:5–8

Dear Lord, I present myself to you again. Transform me by the renewing of my mind, so that I can discern what is the will of God—what is good and acceptable and perfect.

RELATED SCRIPTURE READING—1 PETER 2:1–3

TERESA OF AVILA

(1515–1582)

Let's not think that everything is accomplished through much weeping but set our hands to the task of hard work and virtue. These are what we must pay attention to; let the tears come when God sends them and without any effort on our part to induce them. These tears from God will irrigate this dry earth, and they are a great help in producing fruit. The less attention we pay to them the more there are, for they are the water that falls from heaven. The tears we draw out by tiring ourselves in digging cannot compare with the tears that come from God, for often in digging we shall get worn out and not find even a puddle of water, much less a flowing well. Therefore, sisters, I consider it better for us to place ourselves in the presence of the Lord and look at his mercy and grandeur and at our own lowliness, and let him give us what he wants, whether water or dryness. He knows best. . . . With such an attitude we shall go about refreshed, and the devil will not have so much chance to play tricks on us.

WRITTEN TO CARMELITE NUNS BY TERESA OF AVILA

Here, Spanish mystic Teresa of Avila speaks about weeping, addressing the sisters of her religious order. Perhaps some of them were prone to cry during worship or devotions, or maybe weeping had become a spiritual fad among them. She cautions them not to force their tears, as though this were the only way to worship. We could replace Teresa's words *weeping* and *tears* with other expressions. For example: Let's not think that everything is accomplished through much *praising*; or, The *rejoicing* we draw out by tiring ourselves in digging cannot compare with the *rejoicing* that comes from God. Or substitute *laughter, singing,* and so on.

This is not to say that these things are not desirable. A worshiper may experience all these on one Lord's Day morning—tears may be shed because of personal shortcomings or sin; laughter is evoked by the humor of life; hymns of praise to God are sung in the joy of Christ's redemption. But none of these is required for true worship.

This is exactly what Jesus told the woman at Jacob's well: "The hour is coming, and is now here, when the true worshipers will worship the Father in spirit and truth, for the Father seeks such as these to worship him" (John 4:23). Teresa's advice is in harmony with this truth. She said, "[Let's] place ourselves in the presence of the Lord and look at his mercy and grandeur and at our own lowliness, and let him give us what he wants." Be it tears or laughter, no matter, because God is seeking worshipers who worship "in spirit and truth" (v. 24).

The reverse of this is what Teresa calls "tiring ourselves in digging." Is there anything more dry than self-effort in worship—the attempt to feel joy, the work of praise, the obligation to repentance? Then she describes the alternative to such barrenness: "Let [God] give us what he wants, whether water or dryness. He knows best what is suitable for us. With such an attitude we shall go about refreshed."

The founder of a reformed Carmelite order, the Discalced (barefoot) Carmelites, Teresa of Avila became a nun at the age of sixteen. She experienced a vision of Christ when she was forty and called this her "second conversion."

Teresa worked with John of the Cross in advancing the Catholic Counter-Reformation, which acknowledged many of the abuses the Protestants criticized but attempted to bring about regeneration and reorganization within the Catholic Church itself.

Teresa of Avila's books on the mystical way include *Autobiography* (1562), *The Way of Perfection* (1565), *Book of Foundations*, and *Interior Castle* (1577). These brought her the title Doctor (i.e., teacher) of the Church. Her saintliness and the miracles that were reported to have been done by her led to her canonization in 1622.

Lord Jesus Christ, I offer myself to you. May I worship in spirit and truth. Empty me, I pray, and become in me a spring of water gushing up to eternal life.

RELATED SCRIPTURE READING—1 CORINTHIANS 14:26

JEANNE GUYON

(1648–1717)

Strong are the walls around me,
  That hold me all the day;
But they who thus have bound me,
  Cannot keep God away:
My very dungeon walls are dear,
  Because the God I love is here. . . .

'Tis that which makes my treasure,
  'Tis that which brings my gain;
Converting woe to pleasure,
  And reaping joy from pain.
Oh, 'tis enough, whate'er befall,
  To know that God is all in all.

A POEM BY JEANNE GUYON

John Wesley once said of Madame Guyon, "We may search many centuries before we find another woman who was such a pattern of true holiness."

The French mystic Jeanne Marie Bouvier Guyon, after being widowed in 1676, began traveling extensively throughout France and Switzerland as an apostle of Quietism teaching that spiritual perfection is attained when self is lost in the contemplation of God, the eternal reality. She won disciples and enemies.

In 1686, Guyon became influential at the royal court, but authorities harassed her, burned her books, and charged her with heresy. In 1687 she was confined to a convent and eventually censured by the Vatican.

Then in 1698, Madame Guyon was imprisoned for four years in the infamous Bastille in Paris, placed there by religious authorities who disagreed with her teaching and were jealous of her popularity with the common folk. Her poem describes that experience.

It is said that Adoniram Judson, the heroic American missionary to Burma, consoled himself in a Burmese prison by repeating Guyon's words of love to God:

> No bliss I seek, but to fulfill
> In life, in death, thy lovely will;
> No succor in my woes I want,
> Except what thou art pleased to grant.
> Our days are numbered—let us spare
> Our anxious hearts a needless care;
> 'Tis thine to number out our days,
> And ours to give them to thy praise.

How fitting that someone who suffered as much as Judson would draw strength from Jeanne Guyon, who prayed to God, "In goodness thou hast afflicted me." Guyon believed that tribulation and suffering were necessary to bring a believer the experience of a full inward life with God.

People today are bound by family, chained by finances, shackled by poor health. Each personal prison seems as tight as Guyon's Bastille. But listen to her song: "Oh, 'tis enough, whate'er befall, / To know that God is all in all."

In Colossians Paul says that Jesus Christ is *all in all* (3:11): He is the firstborn of all creation (1:15); all things hold together in him (1:16); all the fullness of God is pleased to dwell in him (1:19); all things are reconciled to God through him (1:20); and all the treasures of wisdom and knowledge are hidden in him (2:3). Though you are imprisoned, Christ is your all in all.

This woman found you, Lord, in prison. So I know that I can find you as well. Increase my faith so I will not see my personal prison but instead have fellowship with you in every episode of my life.

RELATED SCRIPTURE READING—JOHN 20:19

PART 7

THE
WRITERS

HARRIET BEECHER STOWE

(1811–1896)

Legree drew in a long breath; and suppressing his rage, took Tom by the arm, and approaching his face almost to his, said in a terrible voice, "Hark 'e Tom! . . . You've always stood it out agin me: now, I'll conquer ye or kill ye!—one or t'other. I'll count every drop of blood there is in you, and take 'em, one by one, till ye give up!"

Tom . . . answered, "Mas'r, if you was sick, or . . . dying, and I could save ye, I'd *give* ye my heart's blood; and, if taking every drop of blood in this poor old body would save your precious soul, I'd give 'em freely, as the Lord gave his for me. O, Mas'r! don't bring this great sin on your soul! . . . Do the worst you can, my troubles'll be over soon; but, if you don't repent, yours won't *never* end!"

Like a strange snatch of heavenly music, heard in the lull of a tempest, this burst of feeling made a moment's blank pause. Legree stood aghast, and looked at Tom; and there was such a silence, that the tick of the old clock could be heard, measuring, with silent touch, the last moments of mercy and probation to that hardened heart.

It was but a moment.

FROM *UNCLE TOM'S CABIN*

The abolitionist and writer Harriet Beecher Stowe was born in Litchfield, Connecticut, to Lyman and Roxana (Foote) Beecher. Her father, a persuasive preacher and theologian, was a founder of the American Bible Society. All six of her brothers entered the ministry. The youngest, Henry Ward Beecher, was most prominent. Harriet Beecher married the clergyman/professor Calvin Ellis Stowe, and together they had seven children.

Like many Americans in the 1840s, the Stowes became more and more concerned with the abolition of slavery. In 1850

Congress passed the Fugitive Slave Act. This granted slave-holders the right to pursue fugitive slaves into free states. Many citizens in the North and enraged abolitionists rose to greater action. In this climate, in 1852, Stowe published her novel *Uncle Tom's Cabin* (or, *Life Among the Lowly*). Its publication was a watershed event for a nation speeding toward civil war.

Uncle Tom's Cabin sold three thousand copies the first day and three hundred thousand the first year. The book has never gone out of print and is considered one of the most effective pieces of reform literature ever published.

Stowe described herself as "a little bit of a woman, somewhat more than forty, about as thin and dry as a pinch of snuff, never very much to look at in my best days and looking like a used up article now." But this "little bit of a woman" created memorable characters and powerfully portrayed the inhumanity of slavery. She introduced the world to Uncle Tom, a man of strength and moral nerve—a rare black hero in American fiction. Her compelling novel's graphic tale of lives bruised and crushed by slavery pricked the conscience of a nation.

In the portion of the story quoted below, the villain Simon Legree's henchmen, Quimbo and Sambo, have just beat Tom nearly to death. Then comes this exchange:

> "O, Tom!" said Quimbo, "we's been awful wicked to ye!"
>
> "I forgive ye, with all my heart!" said Tom, faintly.
>
> "O, Tom! Do tell us who is *Jesus*, anyhow?" said Sambo. . . .
> The word roused the failing, fainting spirit. He poured forth a few energetic sentences of that wondrous One,—his life, his death, his everlasting presence, and power to save.
>
> They wept,—both the two savage men.

Lord, thank you for all the people who work to bring justice to this world. Strengthen their spirits and embolden their hearts as they labor. And raise up many to do justice and to love kindness and to walk humbly with you.

RELATED SCRIPTURE READING—AMOS 5:14–15, 24

HANNAH WHITALL SMITH

(1832–1911)

If I am walking along the street with a very disfiguring hole in the back of my dress, of which I am in ignorance, it is certainly a very great comfort to me to have a kind friend who will tell me of it. And similarly it is indeed a comfort to know that there is always abiding with me a divine, all-seeing Comforter, who will reprove me for all my faults, and will not let me go on in a fatal unconsciousness of them. . . .

I remember vividly the comfort it used to be to me, when I was young, to have a sister who always knew what was the right and proper thing to do, and who, when we went out together, always kept me in order. . . . I was always made comfortable, and not uncomfortable, by her presence. But when it chanced that I went anywhere alone, then I would indeed feel uncomfortable, for then there was no one near to keep me straight. . . .

You may object, perhaps, because you are not worthy of His comforts. I do not suppose you are. No one ever is. But you need His comforting, and because you are not worthy you need it all the more. Christ came into the world to save sinners, not good people, and your unworthiness is your greatest claim for His salvation.

From *The God of All Comfort* by Hannah Whitall Smith

Born into a strict Philadelphia Quaker household, Hannah Whitall Smith is best remembered for her book *The Christian's Secret of a Happy Life* (1875). She was converted in 1858 under Plymouth Brethren influence, hosted Bible classes for women in her home, and beginning in 1867 conducted with her husband a series of religious meetings in America and Europe.

The last paragraph of this selection from Smith's writing mentions that some people may not feel worthy of receiving God's comfort. Hannah Whitall Smith avers that *no one* deserves any attention from God. Yet some people believe they *do* deserve God's favor.

The Gospel of Luke illustrates both positions in one story: "Two men went up to the temple to pray, one a Pharisee and the other a tax collector. The Pharisee, standing by himself, was praying thus, 'God, I thank you that I am not like other people: thieves, rogues, adulterers, or even like this tax collector.' . . . But the tax collector, standing far off, would not even look up to heaven, but was beating his breast and saying, 'God, be merciful to me, a sinner!'" (Luke 18:10–13).

One of these men seems quite comfortable. The other is obviously not comfortable. But which one is the recipient of God's comfort? The Pharisee is an honorable religious man who seems to have a reserved place in the temple—he is standing by himself. He is thankful for who and what he is and what he is not. The tax collector, on the other hand, has a despised occupation. He receives taxes from the Jews on behalf of the Roman government. And he seems to be ashamed to even enter the temple for prayer—he is standing far off beating his breast in grief. Again, which one is the recipient of God's comfort? Jesus answers: "I tell you, this [tax collector] went down to his home justified rather than the other" (v. 14).

Hannah Smith was grateful that she knew "a divine, all-seeing Comforter, who will reprove me for all my faults, and will not let me go on in a fatal unconsciousness of them." The Pharisee in Luke's story is self-exalted. He is fatally unconscious of his sin. The tax collector is under God's kind comfort because he knows he is a sinner. This knowledge leads him to salvation—the true comfort of God.

Heavenly Father, give me the deep understanding that all have sinned and fall short of your glory. I pray that your righteousness would come through faith in Jesus Christ to all those whom I love.

RELATED SCRIPTURE READING—2 CORINTHIANS 1:3–7

EVELYN UNDERHILL

(1875–1941)

Because mystery is horrible to us, we have agreed for the most part to live in a world of labels; to . . . ignore their merely symbolic character, the infinite gradation of values which they misrepresent. We simply do not attempt to unite with Reality. But now and then that symbolic character is suddenly brought home to us. Some great emotion, some devastating visitation of beauty, love or pain, lifts us to another level of consciousness; and we are aware for a moment of the difference between the neat collection of discrete objects and experiences which we call the world and the height, the depth, the breadth of the living, growing, changing Fact, of which thought, life and energy are parts and in which we "live and move and have our being."

FROM *PRACTICAL MYSTICISM* BY EVELYN UNDERHILL

It has been said that no woman in Christian history has written more than Evelyn Underhill on the meaning and practical value of Christian mysticism. She was born in London, raised an Anglican, and educated at King's College for Women in London. Underhill had many interests such as sailing and bicycling. Her classic work, *Mysticism: A Study in the Nature and Development of Man's Spiritual Consciousness*, an evaluation of spirituality from the early Christian era to the beginning of the twentieth century, was published in 1911.

Highly influential in the Anglican tradition, Underhill devoted herself to social services, speaking at church retreats, and writing, and was the only woman of her generation to be chosen by any Oxford college as an outside lecturer on religion.

Her own life combined ethical living with a deep devotion to God—an example of practical mysticism. To her, the life of a religious person was not to be isolated but rather concerned with the problems of everyday living, especially with the poor.

108

Evelyn Underhill deals with Christian mysticism, contemplation, and the meaning of the mystical life in *Practical Mysticism*. Engagingly she invites the reader to the possibilities of growing more deeply in relationship with God.

In the short paragraph excerpted here, Underhill refers to *mystery* and matches it with *Reality*—the one in whom "we live and move and have our being" (Acts 17:28). Christians live in this wonderful *revealed* mystery: God "has made known to us the mystery of his will, according to his good pleasure that he set forth in Christ" (Ephesians 1:9). Underhill tells us that we usually do not embrace this mystery. Instead we "live in a world of labels."

These labels may be denominational and doctrinal preferences or cultural and racial stereotypes or the lingo and catch phrases used to ease or even erase the meaning of our life's experience. Underhill says that these are merely symbolic of "the infinite gradation of values which they misrepresent." She hopes that Christians will enter a genuine experience of life with God. After all, it was not pointless that "the mystery that has been hidden throughout the ages and generations . . . has . . . been revealed to his saints. To them God chose to make known how great among the Gentiles are the riches of the glory of this mystery, which is Christ in you, the hope of glory" (Colossians 1:26–27).

It is safe to say that everyone will one day encounter "some devastating visitation of beauty, love or pain." Childbirth can bring this, as can sickness, a brush with death, or great grief. At such times the believers in Christ have a unique opportunity: The illusions of the world peel away, the mystery draws near, and "you . . . have the power to comprehend, with all the saints, what is the breadth and length and height and depth, and to know the love of Christ that surpasses knowledge" (Ephesians 3:18–19).

Dear Father, every family in heaven and on earth takes its name from you. I pray that I may be strengthened in my inner being with power through your Spirit; that Christ may dwell in my heart through faith as I am being rooted and grounded in love.

RELATED SCRIPTURE READING—EPHESIANS 3:14–19

EVELYN UNDERHILL

THE CHURCH'S WORSHIP

The worshipping life of the Christian, [while] profoundly personal, is essentially that of a person who is also a member of a group. . . .

The Christian liturgy—taking this word now in its most general sense—is the ordered framework of the Church's [group] worship, the classic medium by which the ceaseless adoring action of the Bride of Christ is given visible and audible expression. . . .

That the living experience of this whole Church, visible and invisible, past and present, stretched out in history and yet poised on God, must set the scene for Christian worship, not the poor little scrap of which any one soul, or any sectional group is capable.

FROM *WORSHIP* BY EVELYN UNDERHILL

Evelyn Underhill was a prolific writer on the spiritual life, an encouraging spiritual director, and a promoter of the retreat movement. Her own spiritual journey was long and painful and, learning to mix mysticism with common sense, she has helped many to grow in faith.

In addition to *Mysticism: A Study in the Nature and Development of Man's Spiritual Consciousness* (1911), Underhill's other writings on the devotional life are *The Mystic Way* (1913), *Practical Mysticism* (1914), and *The Essentials of Mysticism* (1920). Her much praised work *Worship* (1937) is a study in liturgical practices in various church traditions. Through her writing, Underhill established the uniqueness of Christianity. "In the depth of reality revealed by the cross," she wrote, "Christianity stands alone."

One Sunday morning long ago, I was away from home and woke up to the sound of a ringing church bell. The timbre of the bell aroused in me a desire for God. I walked to the nearby church, drawn by my impulse to worship—to express my need for the divine gift of redemption and forgiveness. The preacher, however, spent the service on a pitch for money. I was so deeply disappointed that I left the building and did not reenter a church for years.

God was merciful and I did return. But this experience taught me how to enter a place of worship: First, I enter expecting nothing of others and everything of God. Second, I prepare my own heart to worship God. For this I use a pattern of prayer found in an old hymn: "Come, thou Fount of ev'ry blessing, / Tune *my* heart to sing thy grace." Third, I think the best of others—that they also are there to worship God with a pure heart.

Here is a prayer of mine that expresses Evelyn Underhill's thought that we worship God as a community:

> Father, you are not only mine, but the Father of everyone who believes. By this I grasp, finally, why your Son taught us to say, "Our Father who is in heaven," not "My Father who is in heaven."
>
> Today I pray *our Father*. These two words loose my loneliness and invade my isolation; they unlock the door of time and banish the barrier of space. From the mountainside in Galilee where Christ was asked, "Teach us to pray," through countless lives until mine today, a slender cord is stretching, braided and spliced with the faith of those who call you Father.

Worship is humanity reaching out to the divine. We can do this because Jesus Christ's person and work is complete and satisfying to God. Yes, worship is personal but it is not lonely. As Underhill says, it is a corporate act in which "the ceaseless adoring action of the Bride of Christ is given visible and audible expression."

O God, may the church be like the psalmist's Jerusalem—a city that is bound firmly together, where the tribes go up to give thanks to your name. O God, peace be within her walls.

RELATED SCRIPTURE READING—JOHN 4:19–24

111

SIMONE WEIL

(1909–1943)

Each occurrence, whatever it may be, is like a touch on the part of God; even each thing that takes place, whether it be fortunate, unfortunate or unimportant from our particular point of view, is a caress of God's.

Our soul is constantly clamorous with noise, but there is one point in it which is silence, and which we never hear. When the silence of God comes into the soul and penetrates it and joins the silence which is secretly present in us, from then on we have our treasure and our heart in God; there are only two things piercing enough to penetrate our souls in this way; they are affliction and beauty.

SELECTED SAYINGS OF SIMONE WEIL

The French mystic, social philosopher, and activist in the French Resistance Simone Weil (pronounced *veyl*) was born into a Jewish family in Paris. When she was five, she refused to eat sugar because the French soldiers of World War I had none; and at age six she could quote the French dramatic poet Jean Racine. Weil did not know she was Jewish until she was ten years old, the same year she informed her parents that she had become a Bolshevik and would from then on read only Communist party newspapers.

Entering college, Weil was critical of Marxist thought, though still opposed to capitalist systems of production. She saw a fundamental conflict "between those who have the machine at their disposal and those who are at the disposal of the machine."

You don't often encounter a former Marxist who studied philosophy, classical philology, and science; taught philosophy; was also a social activist; *and* eventually became a believer in Christ. Such was Simone Weil. She picketed for just causes, refused to eat more than the people on relief, and wrote for leftist journals.

These activities often brought the remarkable young woman into conflict with the school boards for whom she worked.

In 1934 Weil took a job for a year in an auto factory because she wanted to learn the psychological effects of heavy industrial labor. There she observed and personally experienced the deadening effect of machines on workers' souls.

The year 1936 brought the Spanish Civil War and Weil joined an anarchist unit training for action near Zaragoza, Spain. Badly scalded by boiling oil, she went to Portugal to recuperate. There in 1938 Weil had the first of her several Christian mystical experiences. Later she named her former social concerns "ersatz divinity."

When the German Army occupied Paris, Weil moved to the south of France and escaped to the United States in 1942. She later worked with the French Resistance in London. There Weil refused to eat more than the official ration in occupied France. This malnutrition combined with overwork caused her physical collapse. She died of tuberculosis.

After the mystical experiences that led Weil to the faith, she focused on an inward spiritual attendance on God whose presence she understood as absolute but not manifest. As a believer, Weil occupied in her own way the place of interface between faith and the world—possessing the social conscience of a grassroots labor organizer and the certainty and humility of a genuine Christian mystic.

Lord Jesus Christ, you are so real, so alive, so very present. I pray that the hunger for truth you put into Simone Weil would be planted into many, many more hearts. Let the people experience what you have promised—"Seek and you will find."

RELATED SCRIPTURE READING—ACTS 17:22–31

JESSIE PENN-LEWIS

(1861–1967)

On the day of Pentecost, the 120 disciples—men and women—were filled in the *spirit,* as the Spirit of God filled the atmosphere, and their tongues were liberated, so that *they themselves* as intelligent personalities, could speak of the mighty works of God as the Spirit gave utterance, *i.e.,* gave them power to speak. . . .

This influx of the divine Spirit into their spirits, not only left their mental powers in full action, but clarified them, and increased their keenness of discernment and power of thought, as seen in the action and the words of Peter, who spoke with such convincing power that through his words—inspired by the Spirit, but *spoken by him* in intelligent clearness of mind—three thousand were convicted and saved, the true influence of God the Holy Spirit being manifested through him. . . .

The "falling upon" of the Spirit (Acts 2), is therefore upon *the spirit,* clothing it with divine light and power, and raising it into union of spirit with the glorified Lord in heaven; at the same time, baptizing the believer into one spirit with every other member of the mystical Body of Christ, joined to the Head in heaven.

FROM *WAR ON THE SAINTS* BY JESSIE PENN-LEWIS

The British writer and conference speaker Jessie Penn-Lewis was born in South Wales. After a private education she became a leader in the British YWCA, spoke at the British Keswick conferences, and influenced the Great Awakening in Wales (1904–1905).

When Welsh revivalist Evan Roberts had a breakdown from overwork at the time of the Great Awakening, Penn-Lewis stepped in to assist those who carried on for him. She observed and ministered to the many people who were caught up in so-called "false fire"—the counterfeit spiritual experiences and other adverse effects of the revival movement. Later she and Roberts collaborated on the book *War on the Saints* (1912), the classic text on the Christian believer's spiritual conflict with the powers of darkness. The book was a direct result of the effects of the Welsh revival.

In the selection excerpted here Penn-Lewis emphasizes that believers are filled by the Holy Spirit in their human spirit, which is a discrete part of the human being. Various portions of the New Testament support this view. For example, 1 Thessalonians 5:23 says, "May the God of peace himself sanctify you entirely; and may *your spirit* and soul and body be kept sound and blameless at the coming of our Lord Jesus Christ"; and Romans 1:9: "For God, whom I serve with *my spirit* by announcing the gospel of his Son . . ." (italics added in both verses).

Penn-Lewis contends that, according to Scripture, when such a filling occurs, the individual does not lose command of faculties. Rather, he or she possesses mental powers that are in full action. The Holy Spirit within has "clarified them, and increased their keenness of discernment and power of thought."

Furthermore, she insists that such an experience of the Holy Spirit will only strengthen the church—the Body of Christ. She writes, "All who are thus liberated and clothed in spirit are 'made to drink of one Spirit' (1 Corinthians 12:13)—the Holy Spirit— who then, through the [spiritual] capacity of each member of the Body, is able to distribute to each the gifts of the Spirit, for effective witness to the risen Head, 'dividing to each one severally even as he will' (1 Corinthians 12:4–11)."

This divine filling is nothing to fear. So each believer can joyfully obey the apostle's admonition: "Do not get drunk with wine, for that is debauchery; but be filled with the Spirit" (Ephesians 5:18).

Lord, the next time I sing a hymn or spiritual song, fill me with yourself as I am making melody to you. Let me be filled with the Spirit and so give thanks to you at all times and for everything.

RELATED SCRIPTURE READING—EPHESIANS 5:18–20

DOROTHY L. SAYERS

(1893–1957)

Let the Church remember this: that every maker and worker is called to serve God *in* his profession or trade—not outside it. . . . The only Christian work is good work well done. Let the Church see to it that the workers are Christian people and do their work well, as to God: then all the work will be Christian work, whether it is Church embroidery, or sewage-farming. As Jacques Maritain says: "If you want to produce Christian work, be a Christian, and try to make a work of beauty into which you have put your heart; do not adopt a Christian pose."

FROM The Mind of the Maker by Dorothy L. Sayers

Dorothy L. Sayers wrote mystery novels featuring the witty and charming Lord Peter Wimsey. She was among the first women to be granted degrees from Oxford University (she graduated in 1920 with a degree in medieval literature) and was a friend of the Oxford writers known as the "Inklings"—J. R. R. Tolkien, C. S. Lewis, Charles W. S. Williams, John Wain, and others.

While in an air-raid shelter during World War II, Sayers read Dante's *Divine Comedy*. Stunned with its greatness, she later translated it into English. Sayers also wrote on Christian themes. Her best-known Christian work is *The Man Born to Be King* (1941)—twelve dramatic episodes in the life of Christ.

One of her finest works is *The Mind of the Maker* (1941), based on the proposition that "every work of creation is threefold, an earthly trinity to match the heavenly"; the creative *idea* being the Father, the creative *energy* being the Word, and the creative *power* being the indwelling Spirit.

Here is how the apostle Paul described the "eternal purpose that [God] has carried out in Christ Jesus our Lord" (Ephesians 3:11): "that through the church the wisdom of God in its rich variety might now be made known to the rulers and authorities in the heavenly places" (v. 10). God's ultimate purpose is not first that our neighbors would know God's wisdom, nor even that the world would know of it. Rather, the church is on the earth to display God's rich wisdom to the rulers and authorities in the heavenly places.

In light of this, how useless it is to adopt a Christian pose! We once knew a man whose business was carpentry. His business card stated that he was a "Christian carpenter." This bothered us. What Dorothy Sayers has written explains why: "The only Christian work is good work well done." Ordinary people can recognize good work and they can also see through someone who adopts a Christian pose. But a person whose content is God does not need to assume such a pose. This is why Paul prays for us to be filled with God:

> I pray that . . . you may be strengthened in your inner being with power through his Spirit, and that Christ may dwell in your hearts through faith, as you are being rooted and grounded in love. . . . so that you may be filled with all the fullness of God.
>
> EPHESIANS 3:16–19

The testimony of the church is invisible, seen by heavenly authorities. So Paul asked God for invisible things—a strong inner being, a heart suited for Christ's indwelling, a solid footing of love; in other words, he asked that we be filled to fullness with God.

When we are such people, we will work in the world as though for God and "all the work will be Christian work, whether it is Church embroidery, or sewage-farming."

Father of Glory, give me a spirit of wisdom and revelation as I come to know you, so that with the eyes of my heart enlightened, I may know what is the hope to which you have called me and what are the riches of your glorious inheritance among the saints.

RELATED SCRIPTURE READING—EPHESIANS 1:15–19

CORRIE TEN BOOM

(1892–1983)

It was in 1844 that Grandfather had a visit from his minister, Dominie Witteveen, who had a special request. "Willem, you know the Scriptures tell us to pray for the peace of Jerusalem and the blessing of the Jews."

"Ah, yes, Dominie, I have always loved God's ancient people—they gave us our Bible and our Savior."

[W]ith this conversation, a prayer fellowship was started, with Grandfather and his friends praying for the Jewish people. . . .

In a divine way that is beyond our human understanding, God answered those prayers. It was in the same house, exactly one hundred years later, that Grandfather's son—my father—and four of his grandchildren and one great-grandson were arrested for helping save the lives of Jews during the German occupation of Holland. . . .

For helping and hiding the Jews, my father, my brother's son, and my sister all died in prison. My brother survived his imprisonment but died soon afterward. Only Nollie, my older sister, and I came out alive.

So many times we wonder why God has certain things happen to us. We try to understand . . . and we are left wondering. But God's foolishness is so much wiser than our wisdom.

FROM *IN MY FATHER'S HOUSE* BY CORRIE TEN BOOM

Cornelia Arnolda Johanna ten Boom was born in Amsterdam, the fifth child of a watchmaker. Corrie learned the watchmaker's craft and also, at age twenty-four, graduated from a local Bible school.

After World War I the ten Booms were foster family to refugee children, missionaries' children, and orphans and were involved in Christian work including ministry to the Jews. Corrie led Bible classes in public schools, taught Sunday school, and organized clubs for young people.

In 1940 Holland was invaded and occupied by the German army. Because the ten Boom family had worked for years in charitable organizations, people turned to them for help. In 1943 they began to hide people who were in danger of arrest by the Gestapo, including Jews seeking refuge from the Holocaust.

On February 28, 1944, the Gestapo raided the ten Boom home. Corrie; her sisters, Betsie and Nollie; her brother, Willem; and their father, Casper ten Boom, were all arrested along with Nollie's son, Peter, and twenty-nine other people. Casper ten Boom died in prison in March; Willem, Nollie, and Peter were soon released. In June Corrie and her sister Betsie were transferred to the Ravensbruck camp in Germany where, near the end of 1944, Betsie died. Corrie was freed from Ravensbruck on January 1, 1945, apparently through an administrative error.

These brief notes are wholly inadequate to convey the inspiration to faith that one can draw from Corrie ten Boom's wartime experiences. Her story must be told and retold as a lesson in courage and faithfulness in God's service. Middle-aged when she was forced into the maw of the Nazi war machine, ten Boom emerged one of the twentieth century's most vital testimonies for our Lord Jesus Christ and she has told this story in many ways in many books, especially *The Hiding Place* (1972).

As the war ended, ten Boom spoke to small groups about her experiences in the concentration camps. In late 1945 she traveled to the United States and spoke at churches, Bible study groups, and conferences. In 1946 ten Boom purchased the former concentration camp at Darmstadt. This was converted into a refuge for ex-prisoners and people displaced by the war. The vitality and reality of Corrie ten Boom's faith caused her to become well-known in evangelical Protestant circles as she visited and preached in dozens of countries.

I come to you, Jesus, the mediator of the new covenant, to simply thank you for the church, the assembly of the firstborn whose names are enrolled in heaven.

RELATED SCRIPTURE READING—HEBREWS 12:22–24

CORRIE TEN BOOM

PAPA'S PRAYER

When we are very young the future is so hard to grasp. My father had one coming event that he mentioned in every prayer. It baffled me. . . .

I waited until Father came upstairs to tuck me in; this was a time I could ask him anything.

"Papa, you always pray in every prayer, 'Let soon come that great day when Jesus Christ, your beloved Son, comes on the clouds of heaven.' Why are you longing for that day?"

". . . The whole world is filled with fighting. You may see worse fighting in your lifetime than what you have seen on the street."

I hoped not. Fighting upset me.

"In the Bible," Papa continued, "we read that Jesus has promised to come to this world to make everything new. The world is now covered with hatred, but when Jesus returns, the world will be covered with the knowledge of God, like the water covers the bottom of the sea."

Thinking of that wonderful day, I knew why Papa prayed for it so often. "Oh, Papa, then everyone will know about Jesus! I'll be very happy when he comes."

FROM *IN MY FATHER'S HOUSE* BY CORRIE TEN BOOM

Corrie ten Boom wrote many books about her life, the work of God, and the love of God. These include, *Plenty for Everyone* (1967), *The Hiding Place* (1972), *Tramp for the Lord* (1974), *Corrie ten Boom's Prison Letters* (1975), and *A Tramp Finds a Home* (1978).

The ten Boom house in Haarlem, the Netherlands, is open to the public—the testimony of a family that lived, labored, and paid the highest price in service to humanity. A watchmaker still works in the home where Corrie grew up and where her father prayed for Christ's soon return.

"What will happen at the second coming of Christ?" This question has been asked since Jesus Christ himself was in Jerusalem: "When he was sitting on the Mount of Olives, the disciples came to him privately, saying, 'Tell us, . . . what will be the sign of your coming and of the end of the age?'" (Matthew 24:3). The remainder of Matthew 24 is given over to a description of the last days—much of it is rather frightening.

This often gives rise to another question: What will happen to *me* at this time? Preachers may use this query to put the fear of God into believers and nonbelievers alike, but the New Testament does not do this. The coming of Christ is the glory of Israel and the hope of all humanity. It is the day when death is swallowed up in Christ's victory.

The question, What will happen to me? may cause fear because no one can make himself or herself truly ready for this tremendous event—except in this way: Cultivate trust in God and nurture love for Christ. With such trust and love we will long for the day of Christ's return (2 Timothy 4:8), watch for it (Luke 12:35–40), wait for it (Philippians 3:20), pray for its fulfillment (Revelation 22:20), look forward to it (2 Peter 3:12–13), and be patient until it arrives (James 5:7–8).

Revelation describes some fearful events at the end of time and concludes with these words: "The one who testifies to these things says, 'Surely I am coming soon'" (22:20a). The response to this promise is *not* one of fear, such as, "O Lord! please make me ready." Rather it is the rejoinder of hope and love: "Amen. Come, Lord Jesus!" (22:20b). As little Corrie ten Boom exclaimed, "Oh, Papa, then everyone will know about Jesus! I'll be very happy when he comes."

Dearest Lord Jesus, I look for the day of your coming when my mortal body will put on immortality. Until then, let me be steadfast, immovable, excelling in your work with this prayer on my lips: "Amen. Come, Lord Jesus."

RELATED SCRIPTURE READING—1 CORINTHIANS 15:50–58

ELIZABETH O'CONNOR

(1921–1998)

> Some of us have looked into the face of our idols and found that one of them is money.
>
> Though we along with millions of other churchgoers are saying that Jesus saves, we ask ourselves if we are not in practice acting as though it were money that saves. We say that money gives power, money corrupts, money talks. Like the ancients with their molten calf we have endowed money with our own psychic energy, given it arms and legs, and have told ourselves that it can work for us. More than this we enshrine it in a secret place, give it a heart and a mind and the power to grant us peace and mercy.
>
> FROM *LETTERS TO SCATTERED PILGRIMS*, 1979

Elizabeth O'Connor was an early member of The Church of the Saviour in Washington, D.C., founded in 1947. She later joined the church's staff and for forty years chronicled the work of the church community. She was a gifted writer, teacher, counselor, and advocate of equality for women, the poor, and the oppressed. In 1984 O'Connor received the honorary degree of Doctor of Humane Letters from the Episcopal Theological Seminary in Alexandria, Virginia.

O'Connor wrote *Letters to Scattered Pilgrims* in response to the needs of the Church of the Saviour. In 1975 the church had grown to the point that communication was breaking down between its members. So, instead of adding more professional staff, the church re-formed itself into six new church communities. O'Connor wrote a series of letters to the new communities. These make up the eleven chapters of *Letters to Scattered Pilgrims*.

In the excerpt quoted here, O'Connor is asking her readers to examine themselves to see if God or money is their real master. This reminds us of the Bob Dylan song "Gotta Serve Somebody." It is a five-verse catalogue of more than thirty types of people—construction worker, preacher, state trooper—on and on. The chorus drives home a basic message of the gospel—no matter who or what you are, you are serving someone. Dylan sings, "It may be the devil or it may be the Lord / But you're gonna have to serve somebody." This idea is so basic that it is included in Christ's message of Matthew 5–7: "No one can serve two masters," he said; "for a slave will either hate the one and love the other, or be devoted to the one and despise the other. You cannot serve God and wealth" (6:24).

Yes, there are only two masters and one is the Lord. As for the other, Genesis says, "The serpent was more crafty than any other wild animal that the LORD God had made" (3:1). This crafty one has devised a most subtle way of gaining human hearts—attachment to money.

But money itself is neutral in this endeavor. As Paul says, "For *the love of money* is a root of all kinds of evil" (1 Timothy 6:10, italics added). This verse continues, "and in their *eagerness to be rich* some have wandered away from the faith." This knocks the legs out from under a common excuse: "I'm not rich, so I'm not serving money." Not many people are truly rich. But many of us are eager to be rich. This is all it takes to draw a person away from the faith, to be "pierced through with many pains."

What to do? Elizabeth O'Connor says, "What if the world is right and there are things that only money can buy, gifts of the spirit that only money can unlock, and blocks that only money can push aside? . . . the answers . . . in the end have to be individual answers, for we are each at a different place in our spiritual trek with different understanding of what the gospel has to say to us about what we do with our money."

Dear Lord Jesus Christ! I know that I cannot serve God and money. And I cannot resist your words. Save me from this perplexing subtlety. Teach me how to daily choose so I may truly hate the one and love you.

RELATED SCRIPTURE READING—LUKE 16:10–15

INDEX AND
SELECTED BIBLIOGRAPHY

Askew, Anne   64
Beilin, Elaine V., ed. *The Examinations of Anne Askew*. New York: Oxford University Press, 1996.

Aylward, Gladys   40
Swift, Catherine. *Gladys Aylward*. Women of Faith Series. Minneapolis: Bethany, 1989.

Blackwell, Antoinette Brown   34
Cazden, Elizabeth. *Antoinette Brown Blackwell: A Biography*. New York: Feminist Press, 1983.
Lasser, Carol, and Marlene Deahl Merrill, eds. *Friends and Sisters: Letters between Lucy Stone and Antoinette Brown Blackwell, 1846-93*. Women in American History. Carbondale: University of Illinois Press, 1987.

Booth, Catherine   20
Booth, Catherine. *For God Alone*. Emerald House Group, 1997.
Hattersley, Roy. *Blood and Fire: William and Catherine Booth and the Salvation Army*. New York: Doubleday, 2000.

Bradstreet, Anne   74, 76
Hensly, Jeannine, ed. *The Works of Anne Bradstreet*. Cambridge: Belknap Press, 1981.
Hutchinson, Robert, ed. *Poems of Anne Bradstreet*. New York: Dover, 1969.
Rimmer, Robert H. *The Resurrection of Anne Bradstreet*. Amherst, N. Y.: Prometheus Books, 1987.

Browning, Elizabeth Barrett   78
Browning, Elizabeth Barrett. *Elizabeth Barrett Browning: Selected Poems*. Edited by Margaret Forester. Baltimore: Johns Hopkins University Press, 1988.
Browning, Elizabeth Barrett. *Sonnets from the Portuguese*. Edited by Julia Markus and William S. Peterson. Hopewell, N.J.: Ecco Press, 1996.
Markus, Julia. *Dared and Done: The Marriage of Elizabeth Barrett and Robert Browning*. New York: Knopf, 1995.

Carmichael, Amy   38
Carmichael, Amy. *Edges of His Ways*. Fort Washington, Pa.: Christian Literature Crusade, 1980.

125

Hildegard of Bingen   88

Bowie, Fiona, and Oliver Davies, eds. *Hildegard of Bingen: Mystical Writings*. Crossroad Spiritual Classics Series. New York: Crossroad, 1990.

Flanagan, Sabina. *Hildegard of Bingen, 1098–1179: A Visionary Life*. New York: Routledge, 1998.

Hildegard von Bingen: Canticles of Ecstasy. Sequentia. BMG/Deutsche Harmonia Mundi—77320. Compact disc.

Hutchinson, Anne   68

Dunlea, William. *Anne Hutchinson and the Puritans: An Early American Tragedy*. Pittsburgh: Dorrance, 1993.

Judson, Ann   54

Brumburg, Jane Jacobs. *Mission for Life: The Judson Family and American Evangelical Culture*. New York: New York University Press, 1984.

Hall, Gordon Langley. *Golden Boats from Burma: The Story of Ann Hasseltine Judson, the First American Woman Missionary in Burma*. Philadelphia: Macrae Smith, 1961.

Julian of Norwich   92, 94

Julian of Norwich. *Revelations of Divine Love*. New York: Penguin Classics, 1999.

Obbard, Elizabeth Ruth. *Introducing Julian, Woman of Norwich*. New Rochelle, N.Y.: New City Press, 1996.

Livingstone, Mary Moffat   56

Nicholls, C. S. *David Livingstone*. International Publications, 1998.

Luther, Katherine Von Bora   48

Marius, Richard. *Martin Luther: The Christian between God and Death*. Cambridge, Mass.: Belknap Press, 1999.

Schreiber, Clara Seuel. *Katherine: Wife of Luther*. Philadelphia: Muhlenberg, 1954.

McPherson, Aimee Semple   36

Epstein, Daniel Mark. *Sister Aimee: The Life of Aimee Semple McPherson*. Eugene, Oreg.: Harvest House, 1994.

Monica   44

Augustine. *Confessions of St. Augustine*. New York: Vintage Classics, 1998.

Christiani, Leon. *Saint Monica and Her Son Augustine*. Boston: St. Paul Books and Media, 1997.

Mother Teresa   24

Kumar, Sunita. *Mother Teresa of Calcutta*. San Francisco: Ignatius Press, 1999.

Rai, Raghu, and Navin Chawla. *Faith and Compassion: The Life and Work of Mother Teresa*. Rockport, Mass.: Element, 1997.

Spink, Kathryn. *Mother Teresa: A Complete Authorized Biography*. San Francisco: HarperSanFrancisco, 1998.

O'Connor, Elizabeth   122

O'Connor, Elizabeth. *Cry Pain, Cry Hope: Thresholds to Purpose*. Potters House, 1993.

O'Connor, Elizabeth. *Letters to Scattered Pilgrims*. San Francisco: Harper and Row, 1979.

126

Penn-Lewis, Jessie   114
Jones, Brynmor Pierce. *The Trials and Triumphs of Jessie Penn-Lewis*. South Plainfield, N. J.: Bridge-Logos, 1997.
Penn-Lewis, Jessie, and Evan Roberts. *War on the Saints*. New York: Thomas E. Lowe, Ltd., 1994.

Rossetti, Christina   82
Rossetti, Christina. *Christina Rossetti: Selected Poems*. Bloomsbury Classic Poetry Series. New York: St. Martin's Press, 1995.
Rossetti, Christina. *The Complete Poems of Christina Rossetti*. Baton Rouge: Louisiana State University Press, 1979.

Sayers, Dorothy L.   116
Loades, Ann, ed. *Dorothy L. Sayers: Spiritual Writings*. Boston: Cowley, 1993.
Reynolds, Barbara. *Dorothy L. Sayers: Her Life and Soul*. New York: St. Martin's Press, 1995.
Sayers, Dorothy L. *The Mind of the Maker*. San Francisco: HarperSanFrancisco, 1941.

Seton, Elizabeth   16
Dirvin, Joseph I. *The Soul of Elizabeth Seton*. San Francisco: Ignatius Press, 1990.

Slessor, Mary   32
Miller, Basil. *Mary Slessor*. Minneapolis: Bethany House, 1985.

Smith, Hannah Whitall   106
Smith, Hannah Whitall. *The Christian's Secret of a Happy Life*. Springdale, Penn.: Whitaker House, 1997.

Smith, Hannah Whitall. *The God of All Comfort*. Springdale, Penn.: Whitaker House, 1997.

Stowe, Harriet Beecher   104
Hedrick, Joan D. *Harriet Beecher Stowe: A Life*. New York: Oxford University Press, 1995.
Stowe, Harriet Beecher. *Uncle Tom's Cabin: Authoritative Text, Backgrounds and Contexts, Criticism*. Edited by Elizabeth Ammons. New York: W. W. Norton, 1993.

Taylor, Maria Dyer   58
Taylor, Howard. *Biography of James Hudson Taylor*. London: Hodder & Stoughton, 1997.

Ten Boom, Corrie   118, 120
Ten Boom, Corrie. *The Hiding Place*. Grand Rapids: Revell, 1996.

Teresa of Avila   98
Bielicki, Tessa. *Teresa of Avila: Mystical Writings*. The Crossroad Spiritual Legacy. New York: Crossroad, 1994.
Medwick, Kathleen. *Teresa of Avila: The Progress of a Soul*. New York: Knopf, 1999.
Teresa of Avila. *Way of Perfection*. Edited by Allison E. Peers. New York: Image Books, 1991.

Truth, Sojourner   28, 30
Painter, Nell Irvin. *Sojourner Truth: A Life, a Symbol*. New York: W. W. Norton, 1997.
Truth, Sojourner. *The Narrative of Sojourner Truth*. Edited by Margaret Washington. New York: Vintage Books, 1993.

Underhill, Evelyn 108, 110

Underhill, Evelyn. *Mysticism: The Nature and Development of Spiritual Consciousness*. Rockport, Mass.: Element, 1999.

Underhill, Evelyn. *Practical Mysticism*. Alpharetta, Ga.: Ariel Press, 1988.

Weil, Simone 112

Little, J. P. *Simone Weil*. New York: St. Martin's Press, 1988.

Plant, Stephen, and Peter Vardy, eds. *Simone Weil*. Great Christian Thinkers. Liguori, Mo.: Liguori Publications, 1997.

Weil, Simone. *Gravity and Grace*. Lincoln: University of Nebraska Press, 1997.

Weil, Simone. *Waiting for God*. New York: Harper Perennial, 1992.

Wesley, Susanna 50, 52

Harmon, Rebecca Lamar. *Susanna, Mother of the Wesleys*. Nashville: Abingdon, 1991.

Wallace, Charles, Jr., ed. *Susanna Wesley: The Complete Writings*. New York: Oxford University Press, 1997.

Whitman, Narcissa 70

Drury, Clifford Merrill, ed. *Where Wagons Could Go: Narcissa Whitman and Eliza Spalding*. Lincoln: University of Nebraska Press, 1997.

Jeffrey, Julie Roy. *Converting the West: A Biography of Narcissa Whitman*. The Oklahoma Western Biographies. Norman: University of Oklahoma Press, 1994.

Margaret Partner, a native of Oregon, is a teacher and storyteller. Daniel, a writer and musician, was born in Colorado. Together, they also wrote *Women of Sacred Song: Meditations on Hymns by Women* (Revell, 1999). Other books recently published by Daniel Partner are *The One Year Book of Poetry* (Tyndale, 1999) and *The Story of Jesus: A Portrait of Christ from the Gospels* (Barbour, 2000). The Partners have four children.